YOU'RE HIRED, MOMMY! THE PROBATION YEAR

Honouring the toughest job in the world — zero training, infinite KPIs.

PALLAVI RAJ

KAUSHVIKA SOULCRAFT CREATION PRIVATE LIMITED

Published by:
Kaushvika Soulcraft Creation Private Limited
BLUERIDGE T-B4 F.NO.1807, RGIP PH-I, Infotech Park (Hinjawadi), Haveli, Pune- 411057, Maharashtra, India.

Paperback-ISBN: 978-81-996201-0-0
Hardcover-ISBN: 978-81-996201-7-9
E-Book-ISBN: 978-81-996201-4-8

To Kaushiki and Saatvika—

Thank you for choosing me as your mother.
This book lives because you lived in my arms, my days and my heart.

Always, always yours.
Mommy

The Voices that made this book more alive:

1. **Dr. Arti Sharma**
2. **Dr. Saakshi Gulati**
3. **Mrs. Divya Dubey**
4. **Mrs. Aradhana Syal**
5. **Dr. Pragya**
6. **Mrs. G Annie Sujitha**
7. **Mrs. Jiggyassa Soni**
8. **Mrs. Shreya Rani**
9. **Mrs. Shreya Kumar Takkalki**
10. **Mrs. Neha Sharma**
11. **Mrs. Anupama Narayanan**
12. **and many more…**

Thank You for trusting me with your stories.

WHO THIS BOOK IS FOR

This is not a parenting guide.
It's not advice.
It's recognition.

If you're reading this feeling overwhelmed, emotional, or simply trying to get through the day—
Come sit for a moment.
Imagine chai on the stove.
Someone finally asking, "Tu theek hai?" and actually listening.

This book is for real mothers—
the ones who wake up early, hold everything together quietly,
break down in bathrooms or balconies,
and still show up again the next morning.

It's also for the new mother surrounded by family, advice, and expectations—
yet feeling unseen while her body and heart are still healing.

This book is for fathers too.
For the men who were taught to provide, not always to notice—
and who learned, sometimes late, how much was being carried without being said.
And yes, this book is for mothers-in-law.
Because once upon a time, you were that exhausted new mother too.

You survived without language for your overwhelm.
Maybe reading this will help you name what you went through.
May it will help you hold the new mothers in your life more gently.

If you're buying this for a friend, expect tears, laughter, and a long hug— followed by one sentence:

"Thank God someone finally wrote this."

Because this story belongs to all of us.
Every mother who survived the year no one warned her about.
Every father who learned to see differently.
Every family trying to do better than the generation before.

This is your story too.

SECTION I: The Start of Journey

Insta Handle: @Sneha.Rohan.Diaries

*Disclaimer: Refer Disclaimer section at the end

CHAPTER 1—
THE JOB SHE DIDN'T APPLY FOR

Long before Sneha became 'Mumma,' 'baby ki mummy,' 'milk machine,' 'sleep hostage,' and 'the woman whose identity was absorbed faster than her postpartum bleeding' –

She was simply **Sneha.**

Sneha who had a job she was secretly good at.
Sneha who hated ladoo's with religious commitment.
Sneha who dreamed of a Bali trip (which her marriage vows silently vetoed).
Sneha who believed marriage was teamwork, not an extended internship with no stipend.
Sneha who ate spicy Momo because life needed flavour – even if pregnancy books said "avoid masala."
Sneha who thought motherhood was a magical promotion— a spiritual stock market that only goes up.

Then came her godh bharai.

Her chachi smushed a ghee-heavy halwa into her palm and declared,
"Congratulations beta, you've been promoted!"

Sneha blinked.
"Promoted to what?"

"To MOTHER! Big big promotion!"

Promotion.
Right.

Except Sneha had no idea what the new job role was,
who the reporting manager would be?
whether it came with health benefits or just haemorrhoids.

Promotions usually come with role descriptions, training manuals, HR Induction, performance benchmarks, and the option to decline if you're not ready.

This came with ghee, expectations, and absolutely no exit clause.

The living room buzzed with sarees, bangles and opinions.
Someone tied a dupatta around her head like she'd just been crowned Miss Bharat Janani.
A cousin whispered mantras for easy labour.
A neighbour argued whether the baby's nose should come from Sneha or Rohan.
Sneha prayed the baby didn't inherit either of their foreheads.
Meanwhile, Rohan floated around like a helium balloon with a front-camera obsession.

Selfies with aunties.
Photos with Sneha's belly.
Accepting compliments like he had personally assembled the foetus with Fevicol and determination.

Every congratulation felt like a LinkedIn endorsement for a job she hadn't interviewed for.

And beneath his proud grin were the wires of every Indian 90s boy.
Bring money.
Wife handles everything else.

Not a villain.
Just a product of "Well-meaning Patriarchy Manufacturing Plant Pvt. Ltd."

Sneha smiled anyway.
She liked her life – weekend brunches, corporate deadlines, and the ability to poop in silence.
No one warned her that motherhood was an exchange offer:

Give us your identity, sleep, breasts, career rhythm, sanity and personal space.
In return: **Screaming potato.**

"But who reads fine print at a baby shower?
You can't complaint, or you're ungrateful.
You can't quit, or you're selfish.
You can't ask for help, or you're weak.
But somehow – somehow— you're supposed to be 'naturally' good at this. As if growing a human, birthing a human, and keeping a human alive 24/7 is something women just know how to do.
Like breathing.
Like blinking.

Like it doesn't require seventeen new skills you've never learned."

The Delivery – Also Known As "The Onboarding Without Orientation"

"You did it!" the nurse announced, placing a red, angry, screaming bundle on Sneha's chest.

Sneha waited for the fairytale moment.
Violins.
Sparkles.
A close-up of tearful smiles.

Instead, her brain whispered,
"Why is he purple? Is he supposed to be this purple?
Why is his head shaped like a brinjal that lost a fight?"

Rohan cried harder than the baby.

"She's perfect," he sobbed.

"She? Rohan, he is a boy."

"Oh."
He wiped his tears on his new #1 Dad T-shirt.
"He's perfect."

Within hours, relatives started arriving like back-to-back Amazon orders.

"Look at his forehead!"
"Look at his nose!"
"Thank god he didn't get Sneha's frizzy hair!"
"Arre beta, smile! Happiest day of your life!"

It was and the photo later showed her glowing too.
In reality, it was sweat + shock + injection side effects.

Nobody asked how Sneha was feeling.
Only the baby mattered.
Sneha was the packaging material.

She felt like a courier box everyone inspected and then forgot. Engrossed in what came out of it.

That night, when the room finally emptied, a nurse walked in with a checklist longer than a government tender:

Feed every two hours.
Burp.
Track diapers.
Call if latch fails.
Keep warm.
Watch jaundice.
Relax.

Sneha nodded like an IAS aspirant.
Inside, she was screaming:
"IS THERE A TRAINING MODULE? A TRAILER? A DEMO VERSION?"

Too late.

She had already been hired.

The Terms, Conditions & The Lies We Tell New Moms

Back home, a myth quietly took shape.

"You're such a natural, beta," her mother-in-law chirped, watching Sneha fumble with a diaper like it was an origami exam.

Natural?
If motherhood was natural, why did her nipples feel like they were being used as a chew toys?
Why did her baby scream like an Indian Idol finalist during night shows?

Sneha learned his cries like notification tones:

Eeeeeh-eh-eh → Hungry
AaAAaaaaAa → Gas
Banshee scream → Because chaos is fun
Silent-stare cry → Planning something suspicious

Meanwhile, society asked Rohan:
"How's fatherhood? Proud?"

Society asked Sneha:
"Are you feeding him every two hours?
Is your milk enough?
Is he getting full, is your milk sufficient?

Are you eating right?
Sleeping? (Haha, of course not.)"
Nobody asked,
"How are YOU, beta?"

Her stitches hurt.
Her breasts throbbed.
Her hormones crashed.
Her identity evaporated.

But to everyone else, Sneha was just… default.

Meanwhile, Rohan strutted around like a Rajshri Production hero.

He helped "sometimes."
Folded two towels and waited for applause.
Tried changing a diaper once and Googled "how to know if baby is done pooping" and fainted at the first image.

A modern patriarch – not evil, just conveniently oblivious.

The 4AM Truth

One night, after twelve failed attempts to put the baby down, Sneha sat on the floor at 4 AM, breastfeeding again, tears silently falling.

"I can't do this," she whispered.

Rohan turned over and mumbled,

"Babies are like that only…"

Sneha stared at him.

Of course, babies are like that.
But why must mothers be superhuman?

And then something cracked open— a tiny, rebellious thought:

What if I'm not the problem?

What if the JOB DESCRIPTION is impossible?

What if the myth is wrong – not me?

A window.
A breath.
A beginning.

Her First Tiny Act of Rebellion

The next morning, Sneha did something mildly scandalous.

She ate spicy food.
Not "for baby."
For HER.

The baby didn't explode.
The Earth didn't tilt.
Universe remained intact.

A tiny, delicious rebellion.

Her inner voice whispered: "If I can eat Paneer Tikka guilt-free, maybe I can reclaim the rest of me too."

The Marriage Equation (Or Lack Thereof)

Rohan's life didn't change much.

He still went to gym at fixed times.
Still napped without guilt.
Still expected dinner magically.
Still travelled for work (aka mini- vacations).
Still enjoyed uninterrupted toilet time – a luxury Sneha considered mythical.

He believed bringing money home was The Ultimate Husband Contribution— the gold medal of marriage.

Well-meaning, mildly narcissistic, trained by patriarchy, and blissfully unaware of female exhaustion.

Sneha wasn't trying to change him overnight—
She was learning to speak instead of silently swallowing the resentment that was eating her alive.

The Moment She Finally Spoke

One evening, between feedings and frustration, Sneha looked at Rohan and said, quietly but firmly:

"I don't need help, Rohan.
I need a partner."

For the first time, he didn't argue.
He listened.
Something shifted.

Not much.
But enough.

Evolution doesn't come with fireworks.
It comes with small moments of clarity.

The Truth This Book will Tell

This isn't the story of Mother India.
Not the story of Instagram mommies.
Not the story of women who "manage everything effortlessly."

This is the story of Sneha—
Ambitious.
Messy.
Overwhelmed.
Funny.
Angry.
Soft.
Breaking and rebuilding.

Loving hard.
Surviving harder.

A woman learning:
You can't change the system overnight,
But you can equip yourself with tools, voice, boundaries, and support.

And sometimes that begins with the smallest rebellion—
Eating spicy food, saying "I need help," or telling society, "No, aunty, I'm not glowing. It's sweat."

Sneha's journey starts here.
And it won't be pretty.
But it will be honest, real and overflowing with every emotion— delight, overwhelm, grace, irritation, and the refined art of pretending you're fine when you're two minutes from losing it.

CHAPTER 2—
THE DAY SNEHA WENT MISSING

(A Missing-Person Case with No FIR, No Suspects, and No Intention of Returning Her)

Sneha didn't vanish with the drama of a crime thriller.
No suspense music.
No muddy footprints near the kitchen.
No neighbour peeking over balconies whispering:

"Have you seen this woman? Last seen in maternity leggings and less hope than when Netflix asks, 'Are you still watching?"
Her disappearance was quieter.
Softer.
More…motherly.

One minute she existed.
The next, she had been absorbed – fully, seamlessly—
into the never-ending vortex of burp cloths, half-washed bottles, and a newborn glued to her like she was the last emotional support pillow on earth.

But the real disappearance?

It didn't happen at home.

It happened in the **operation theatre,** under tube lights bright enough to expose her soul.

The OT: The First Time Sneha Felt Herself Slipping Away

Nothing in Sneha's lifetime of moral policing—
not the "beta, cover yourself,"
not the "girls don't sit like that,"
not the entire izzat curriculum prepared her for the moment she'd lie half-naked on a metal table under tube lights bright enough to interrogate criminals, while ten strangers moved around her like her body was a **public workstation at a railway waiting room.**

Sneha lay there,
waist- down numb,
gown migrating upward like it had other plans,
her modesty abandoned somewhere near the ECG machine blinking like,
"Girl, you're on your own today."

A nurse said, "Lift your leg."
Another. "Shift down."
A third: "little more."
Little more?
If she slid little more, she'd fall off the table, deliver the baby on the floor, and donate her last surviving sliver of dignity to medical science.

Amidst this a nurse said, "Madam, do you want mantra? Gayatri? Vishnu Sahastranama?"
She wanted to say shut up, let me focus. But DJ amma already played the mantra…
"Good Maa, Good for baby!!."

The doctor— steady, serene, borderline bored—
asked, "So, what do you want? Boy or girl?" As if Sneha was ordering dosa toppings.

At the foot end, the paediatrician stood ready with a towel, calm as a wicketkeeper waiting for a straightforward catch.

Around her, the room vibrated with **Dadar fish market energy—**
metal clinks, slipper scrapes, snaps of gloves, the thunk of trays, machines beeping like impatient customers.

Not casual chit-chat.
A full-blown, buzzing, efficient, terrifying ballet.
Both outside and within. Something was shifting.

Later that night, in the quite after, Sneha would realise—
It wasn't the pain that stayed with her.

It was the absurd speed at which her body changed status.

One minute, her whole life had been an izzat syllabus.
Cover up. Sit properly. Don't show. Don't invite attention.

The next—
"Leg up."
"Shift down."
"Little more."

Her body, once treated like family gold, had now become just another patient ID scribbled between two emergency cases and a tea break.

And nobody flinched.
Nobody averted their eyes.
Nobody whispered.
Nobody cared.

The same culture that panics over a slipping dupatta had no problem conducting a full committee meeting around her exposed body.

Sacred earlier.
Public now.

Either way— never really hers.

Lying there under the interrogation lights and unsolicited mantras, Sneha felt the feminist explosion quietly ignite inside her.

Not rage.
Not liberation.

Clarity.

They were never protecting women's bodies.
They were managing them.

When her body was young and unmarried—
It was "sacred."
When it was pregnant, useful, producing –
It was public property.

Different labels.

Same control.

It scorched deeper than the epidural. Humiliating and freeing at the same time. A strange clarity wrapped in a hospital sheet.

Because in that moment Sneha realised:
She wasn't her body.
She wasn't her izzat.
She wasn't the rules that caged her.

She was a woman doing the hardest job on earth.

And somewhere between the chaos and the calm professionalism of it all, a version of her slipped away—
And a sharper, clearer one took her place.

The Tuesday She Officially Went Missing (10:32 A.M.)

Weeks later, Sneha stood in her kitchen wearing a faded dress with a baby spit-up stain shaped exactly like the map of Kerala.

The sun was aggressively bright.
Her tea tasted like sadness.
Her spine felt like it had filed for early retirement.

But the house— miracle of miracles – was silent.

The baby slept.
Rohan was at work.

The pressure cooker was taking a break from terrorism.

For the first time in weeks, the silence was loud enough for her to hear…herself.

She looked around and thought:

Where am I?

Not physically.
Physically she was between the fridge and the sink.
Emotionally?
Existentially?
Internally?

She had no idea.

She knew where the pacifiers were.
Where the backup pacifiers were.
Which burp cloth smelled faintly of God's grace and which one smelled of regret.

But she had no clue where she was.

The Phone Call That Explained Nothing (And Everything)

Her phone buzzed.

Mummyji Calling.

Sneha straightened her T-shirt instinctively—
because conditioning kicks in faster than caffeine. She like Shankar Madhavan singing breathless in one breath asked—

"How's the baby?"
"Did he poop?"
"Did he drink milk?"
"Did you burp him?"
"Is he cold?"
"Is he warm?"
"Are you massaging him"
"Show me his face."

It hit her harder than DTC bus.

Before the baby, everyone had advice like they were running an Ayurveda helpline:
"Eat this – good for baby."
"Drink that – good for baby."

After Baby— Eat this, Eat that— "Methi laddoo, jeera water, moringa soup— good, good, good."
But nobody ever asked, "Sneha, beta how are YOU? Do you like the taste? What you want?"

It was like being promoted from "incubator" to "customer care executive."
When the call ended, Sneha finally felt the hit:

Everyone wanted updates on baby, but she – She wanted someone to ask about the woman holding him together.

The Woman on The Fridge

She opened the fridge.

Inside:

One lonely roti.
A traumatised curd packet.
A green chilli fighting for relevance.

And a photo – stuck under a "Follow Your Dreams" magnet.

The girl in the picture?

Bold lipstick.
Smooth hair.
Relaxed posture.
Coffee in hand.
A smile that hadn't been replaced by survival mode.

That woman had time.
That woman had confidence.
That woman had eight-hour sleep cycles.
That woman who took long peaceful showers.
Sneha touched the photo lightly.

"Where did you go?" she whispered.

The fridge, as always, had no interest in solving women's problems.

The Great Identity Rebrand

Sneha didn't realise when it happened.

One day she was "Sneha – project manager, spreadsheet queen, woman with hopes and hobbies."

The next day she was:

Sneha (Mumma) – 24/7 caretaker, feeder, burper, coordinator, emotional shock absorber.
No Sundays. No Salary. No Performance appraisal.

Even Amazon joined in:

Recommended for you, Mumma:
Breast pads, nipple creams, silicone teethers, colic remedies, and a book titled "How Not to Lose Your Mind Before the Baby Turns One."

Overnight, Motherhood Private Limited acquired all shares Sneha Enterprises.

And the Chairman of the Board – Rohan – continued living his work-life balance like the merger didn't affect him.

The Group Chat That Broke Her Hope

"Goa trip in March?"
"YESSSSSS!"
"Booked! Sneha, you coming???"

Sneha stared at the screen.

Coming??
With whom??
Her left boob or her right?

She typed,
"Newborn…can't."

She meant,
"I haven't peed alone in three weeks. Goa is basically Narnia."

The Mirror Incident

After yet another spit-up attack, Sneha washed her face and glanced up.

The woman staring back had:

Dark circles doing a permanent internship,
a bun shaped like a wildlife sanctuary,
and a nursing gown big enough to store all her emotional trauma.

Her eyes looked dimmer.

Her soul looked tired.

"I miss me," she whispered.

It wasn't vanity.
It was grief.

The Balcony Breakdown

That evening, after rocking the baby for an eternity, Sneha stepped onto the balcony – motherhood's version of a panic room.

Outside, life moved.
People moved.
The world moved.

Sneha didn't.
A neighbour waved.
"How's the baby?"

Sneha mouthed, "Fine."

Because that is the only acceptable answer for mothers.

She slid to the floor and cried – quiet tears, leaking slowly, like a woman evaporating without witnesses.

Rohan Enters – With The Wrong Energy

At 10:45 p.m., Rohan entered smelling of corporate AC and freedom.

"How was your day?" he asked casually, scrolling his phone.

Sneha blinked.
Her day?

She had nursed a baby, lost herself, misplaced her sanity, forgotten food and time and everything except survival.

"Same," she said.

He nodded and scrolled reels.
And something tightened inside her—
not anger,
not resentment,
just the loneliness of being unseen.

He was the same.

She was not.

The Moment Of Awareness

At midnight, lying between a snoring husband and a snorting newborn, Sneha stared at the ceiling fan spinning like her thoughts.

And suddenly – with painful clarity – she understood:

She hadn't become a mother.
She had gone missing.

Quietly.
Softly.

Without witnesses.
Without alarms.

And nobody had noticed.

Not even her.
Not until now.

She realised missing wasn't a thriller, it was a clerical error. The world had simply re-assigned her role without waiting for her signature…

CHAPTER 3—
THE PERFECT MOM TRAP

(Or, How Sneha Signed Up for an Expectations Marathon without Noticing the Starting Gun)

The Perfect-Mom Trap never announces its entry.
It doesn't arrive like a dramatic villain in a 90s movie, wind blowing, background music swelling.
It sneaks in quietly—
wrapped in "advice,"
disguised as "concern,"
delivered by aunties who consider judgement a public service.

Sneha fell straight into it—
unknowingly, unwillingly,
while holding mashed banana in one hand
and the thinning edges of her identity in the other.

It began on a perfectly normal afternoon—
where the baby rejected banana puree with the grace and precision of a seasoned Odissi dancer.

Sneha sighed.
The baby turned away.
She sighed louder.
The baby turned further away.
It was a battle she was destined to lose.

And right on cue—
Ding-dong.

The bell that could ruin even the strongest mother's mental stability.

Then came the unmistakable, self-declared introduction:
"Arre Sneha, open the door, beta! It's me!"

Only one woman in the entire complex announced herself like a courier box with COD:

Shobha Aunty.
Local gossip engine.
Self-appointed President of the Motherhood Compliance Board.

Sneha's spine straightened.
Her soul quietly evacuated her body for safety (as trained in Workspace Emergency Response Training)

Aunty Audit Committee— Full Inspection Mode

Shobha Aunty marched in wearing a bright pink saree and judgement stronger than the jasmine oil in her hair.

"Oho! Banana? Why banana? Give apple. Banana constipates."

Sneha inhaled deeply.
Exhaled slowly.
Tried not to throw the bowl into another dimension.
"Actually, doctor said—"

"Doctors!" Aunty scoffed rolling her eyes so hard she nearly strained a muscle.
"These days they don't know anything. In our time –"

Sneha's spirit briefly took a sabbatical above the ceiling fan, and tried filing a complaint against unsolicited advice.

Aunty continued her forensic sweep of the room.

"Why is he not wearing socks? Babies feel cold. Stomach will get upset. Even you are not covering your ears. These days you girls don't listen."

"It's 31 degrees," Sneha replied.

"Yes, but babies feel cold in AC."

"The AC is off."

"Still!"

Sneha considered lighting an agarbatti – not sure whether to summon patience or ghosts. She was open to either.

Before leaving, Aunty delivered her signature 'final blow,' the line she'd sharpened over decades:

"Motherhood is not that hard, beta. Just be more organised."

Sneha smiled.
Closed the door politely.

Then muttered,
"Perfect. I'm failing at feeding banana."

Little did she know—
this was only Level 1 of the Perfect-Mom Trap.

Instagram: Home Of The Unreal

That night, in a moment of pure emotional weakness, Sneha made the fatal mistake of opening Instagram.

First reel:
A pastel-saree mom surrounded by sunshine, sparkles, and a baby who looked Photoshopped by angels.

Caption:
✨ Every moment is magic ✨
#Blessed #MomLife #Gratitude

Sneha tilted her head.
Where was the spit-up?
Where was the 4-hour-long crying session?
Where was the exhaustion?
Where was the real baby?

Next reel:
A mother doing yoga with her baby perched on her shins like a circus act.

Sneha glanced at her own baby, who couldn't even sit straight and frequently collapsed sideways like a drunk uncle at a sangeet.

Next reel:
A mompreneur launching an organic toddler snack brand from her balcony.

Sneha was thrilled because she brushed her teeth at **4 p.m.**

She slammed the app shut. Dropped the phone face down... Picked it...

Sneha reluctantly opened Instagram.

Not to scroll.
To POST.

Her finger hovered over the camera icon.

She looked around.

The house was a disaster. The baby was finally asleep but looked like he'd fought a war (milk crust in his eyebrows, mysterious stain on his onesie). Sneha's hair was...optimistic at best.

She took a photo anyway.

No filter. No angle. No staging.

Just: reality. The she wrote:

Caption:
"Real talk: Motherhood is hard today.
The baby cried for three hours straight.
I haven't showered in two days.
I ate three biscuits and called it lunch.
The house looks like a crime scene.
And I'm so tired I can't remember if I've brushed my teeth.
Is this what they meant by 'cherish every moment'?

Because I'm not cherishing. I'm SURVIVING.
If you're also just surviving today – hi. You're not alone."

She Stared hovering her Finger over "SHARE."

What if people judge?

What if her cousin's screenshot and forward it to family group?

What if everyone thought she was a bad mother?

What if—

She hit post before the fear could win.

Then immediately regretted it.

Locked her phone.

Put it face-down. Anxiously Twitching.

Walked away.

Checked it three minutes later.

----

12 likes.

Then 47.

Then 93.

Comments:

@Priya_mom41: "THANK YOU for being real. I'm crying reading this."

@neha.bangalore: "This is me every day. Why does no one talk about this??"

@ruchi_parenting: "You're a terrible mother for posting this. Babies sense your negativity. Delete this."

@Kavita_newmom: "Ignore that comment above. You're doing Great. I'm in month 2 and barely alive."

@Sarita_Singh (Sneha's MIL): "Beta, why are you sharing private family things online? What will people think?"

Sneha laughed— a tired, slightly unhinged laugh.

There it was.

The Split.

Half the comments: "THANK YOU for being honest."

Half the comments: "How DARE you."

And that's when she felt The Perfect-Mom Trap tightened another notch.

The Perfect- Mom Police were everywhere.

They lived in her head, her house, her family, Instagram, WhatsApp groups.

Making mothers feel guilty for being human.

There were other comments—

@reshma_NewMomLife: "I thought I was the only."
@DP_MOMinMumbai: "feed, burp, sleep, repeat…my life"

Sneha read through them slowly.
She replied to every single one.

Not with Advice, just with:
"You are not alone."

Because that's what she'd needed to hear.

And if her honesty helped even ONE mother feel less isolated—

Worth it.
The judgement will come. She would manage.
She'd survived worse.

The Checklist They Give You vs The Checklist You Actually Need

THEY TELL YOU	YOU ACTUALLY NEED
▪ Sleep when baby sleeps	✓ Permission to cry
▪ Accept help gracefully	✓ Permission to NOT know
▪ Bond with baby immediately	✓ Permission to be angry
▪ Enjoy every moment	✓ Permission to miss your old life
▪ Bounce back quickly	✓ Permission to be human

The difference?
One checklist makes you feel guilty.
The other might save you.

The Projectile Incident – The Exact Moment The Pastel Fantasy Died.

The next morning, Sneha decided she would TRY.
Truly.
Seriously.
Spiritually.

Be calmer.
Be softer.
Be more zen.

Maybe even be one of those "soft-focus moms" who whisper sweet things and manage chaos with grace.

She placed the baby on the changing mat.
Fresh diaper ready.
Wipes ready.
Her optimism dangerously high.

Today was The Day.

Then the baby gave her a suspiciously sweet smile.
The kind of smile villains give before pressing the detonator.

And then—
WHOOSH.

A fountain of projectile pee shot into the air, making perfect contact with her cheek, jaw, collarbone, and brand-new T-shirt.

It splashed with the confidence of a national monument fountain.

A single drop rolled down her nose with artistic commitment.

Sneha froze.
Closed her eyes.
Counted to ten slowly.

Footsteps approached.

Rohan stood at the doorway.

And then…he **snorted.**
Actually snorted.
"Arre yaar, why didn't you cover it?"

Sneha wiped her face slowly—
like a queen preparing for revenge.

"You come here. And say that again."

Rohan's smile died instantly.

Even the baby paused in admiration.

With that moment—
Sneha's pastel-saree Instagram-mom delusion crumbled into dust.

The Family Feedback Committee

Sunday arrived—
and with it, the compulsory pilgrimage to Rohan's parents' house.

Within minutes of arrival, the Family Audit Panel activated:

MIL: "Baby looks thin. Are YOU eating properly?"
FIL: "Why doesn't he sleep on time?"
Sister-in-law. "Follow this influencer – her routine is amazing!"

Sneha nodded mechanically.
Smiled politely.
Internally did full Garba.

Then Rohan proudly declared:

"Sneha manages everything!"
Sneha turned.
Slow.
Dramatic.
Bollywood-level slow motion.

Everything?
Not WE?
Not TOGETHER?
Not SHARED?

Just Sneha?
The household's motherboard?
The emotional-support infrastructure?

She swallowed her irritation like a tablet – bitter, necessary and largely ineffective.

Another notch tightened.

The Voice That Does Not Shut Up

That night, while bouncing the baby, the inner critic began its rave party:

"You weren't patient enough."
"You should've cleaned the house."
"You should've cooked fresh food."
"You should sleep-train."
"You should play more."
"You should smile more."
"You should be perfect."

Sneha whispered,
"Can you PLEASE shut up?"

The voice responded,
"You can't even shut me up."

The Stupid Sentence That Broke Her

Later that week, Rohan walked in, looked around, and casually said:

"Why is the house messy today?"

Sneha stopped breathing.

TODAY?
As opposed to when?
Yesterday, when the house looked like a cyclone zone?
Last week when the sofa hosted a laundry mountain?

Her patience snapped like a cheap rubber band.

"What do you think I DO all day?" she exploded.

Rohan blinked, confused, overwhelmed, unprepared.

"You are at home, you have help, you can manage this much with baby… they anyways sleep around 18 hours rt.
But Sneha was already crying.
Tears of exhaustion.
Tears of being unseen.
Tears of carrying the invisible load alone.

He stepped toward her and froze for a second – he recognised that look, the warning sign every husband learns too late. One wrong word and this wouldn't be a conversation, it would be a volcanic event. So he did the only safe, sane thing left:

Hugged her clumsily and said, "I'm sorry," he whispered.

Of course he didn't understand.
How would he?
No one had ever shown men the backend code of motherhood.

Sneha felt something shift—
not forgiveness.
not anger.

Something quieter.

Understanding?
Maybe.

Maybe not.
But something moved.

2:40 A.M. Realisation

Later that night, breastfeeding in the dark, half-asleep and half-dreaming, Sneha had her moment of clarity.

All these "perfect moms" she envied?
The aunty-critics?
The influencer super-achievers?
The women who seemed sorted?

None of them lived her life.
None carried her mental load.
None rocked her baby at 2:40 a.m.

She whispered:
"Maybe I don't have to be perfect."

Just like that—
a hairline fracture appeared in the Perfect-Mom Trap.

Small.
Silent.
Liberating.

Sneha's First Revolutionary Act

The next morning, Sneha did something bold.

She made herself a cup of hot chai.
Sat down.
And drank it.

HOT.
SLOW.
WITHOUT INTERRUPTION.

The laundry waited.
The sink waited.
The world did not collapse.

With every sip, she felt a warmth spreading inside her—
not the chai's warmth.
Her own.

For the first time in weeks, Sneha wasn't performing.
Wasn't pleasing.
Wasn't chasing perfection.

She was just…**Sneha.**

A tiny rebellion.
A quiet beginning.
The first crack in a system designed to break mothers.

What she didn't know—
not yet—
was that this small act would eventually lead her to question everything.
everything.
her identity,

her marriage,
her ambitions,
and one day soon…

whether she even wanted to go back to the job that once defined her.

But that was for another chapter.
For now—
she took another long sip.

And exhaled. For a glorious minute, the world belonged only to her and her hot cup.

CHAPTER 4—
THE INVISIBLE LOAD

(Or, Why Sneha's Brain Operates Like a Crowded Local Even When She's Sitting Still)

The first time Sneha realised she was carrying the "Invisible Load," it didn't happen during a TED Talk, a parenting webinar, or an Instagram infographic titled Mental Load 101.

It happened because a grown man couldn't find a pair of socks.

Sneha was standing in the living room at **8:17 a.m.,** holding the baby in one arm, a bottle in the other, and mentally calculating whether the diaper stash would last till Sunday or trigger a national emergency.

Rohan walked out of the bathroom with wet hair, a towel, and the confused expression of a man who'd misplaced both his phone and his common sense.

"Sneha...where are my socks?"

Sneha turned slowly, like a CCTV camera detecting criminal behaviour.

"Which socks?" she asked.

Rohan blinked. "My socks?"

"Oh. YOUR socks. The ones YOU wear. On YOUR feet. The ones YOU took off yesterday and kept in YOUR drawer? Those?"

He considered this new information with the seriousness of a man decoding the Mahabharata.

"…Yes?"

"Try the drawer, Rohan," she said calmly— too calmly.

He left.

And Sneha whispered to the baby,
"He has no idea."

Not about socks.
Not about diapers.
Not about mental tabs.
Not about emotional bandwidth.
Not about the thousand tiny decisions that lived rent-free in her mind.

He thought this was a sock problem.

It wasn't.

It was a **headspace problem.**

The Invisible Mental Excel Sheet

Sneha placed the baby down and closed her eyes.

Inside her mind, the invisible Excel sheet whirred to life:

- Doctor appointment – Tuesday
- Vaccination- next week
- Refilling detergent – urgent
- Wipes – 1.5 days left
- Diapers – panic threshold approaching
- Gas cylinder warning
- Milkman payment
- Sterilize bottle
- Sterilize pump
- Sterilize her soul
- Laundry
- Tummy time
- Cooking
- "Where is my left Sanity?"
- Maid on leave
- Medicine stock low
- Did he eat?
- Did he burp?
- So on…

And then came **the Motherhood Bonus Questions:**

Should I pump now?
Do I have enough milk?

Why is latch failing?
Where is the pumping flange?
Why does pumping feel like an audition for Amul's dairy division?
Did I sterilize that bottle or dream it?
Why does everything leak? Bottle? Baby? Boobs? Me?
Will the aunty committee judge me if I bottle-feed?

Sneha exhaled

She wasn't running a home.
She was running:

- a startup
- a logistics company
- a dairy plant
- a hospital
- a cleaning service
- a customer helpline
- a therapy centre
- and a circus

Except she was the **founder, intern, HR, finance, janitor, counsellor and Chief Lactation Officer.**

Meanwhile, Rohan was very proud of washing one **bottle** last night.

One.
Bottle.

Even the baby contributed more – he produced three dirty ones daily.

Where It Actually Began

Sneha realised the invisible load didn't begin with motherhood.

It began with her mother.

Always waking early.
Packing tiffins.
Finding socks.
Tracking bills.
Maintaining peace.
Remembering birthdays.
Anticipating needs.
Being the home's emotional shock absorber.

Her father?

Went to office.
Returned.
Read newspaper.
Asked, "Khana bana?" with the same tone one uses for weather updates.

Sneha's mother never complained.
Never asked for help.
Never called her labour-*labour*.

And like every Indian daughter Sneha inherited this legacy of silent responsibility like family gold.

Except this jewellery weighed 200kilos and came with **zero resale value.**

Sneha looked at her sleeping son and whispered:

"You will NOT grow up thinking this is only a mother's job. Not on my watch."

But to break something this old…
She needed a partner.

And her partner was still asking about socks.

Rohan's Definition Of "Helping"

That evening, Rohan entered the kitchen with the confidence of a man expecting the Bharat Ratna.

"Need help?" he asked, holding a single feeding bottle like it was a trophy.

Sneha stared.

She had:

- washed ten bottles
- sterilised six
- pumped twice

- cooked dal
- wiped the floor
- soothed meltdowns
- and mentally calculated three different versions of failure

But Rohan washed **one** bottle.

And expected applause.

"Rohan," she said quietly,
"I don't need HELP.
I need PARTNERSHIP."

He blinked. "Same thing, no?"

"No.
Help is optional.
Partnership is responsibility."

His brain started buffering.
He opened his mouth, closed it, rebooted.
"…Okay."

He meant it.
He didn't understand it.
Not yet.

The Baby's Vomit — God's Equaliser

Just then, the baby burped.

Sneha relaxed—fatal error.

A sudden white waterfall of projectile vomit hit Rohan's shirt with Olympic precision.

Rohan froze.
Sneha folded her arms.

"He vomited ON me!" he gasped.

She nodded.
"Welcome. To my office."

He looked horrified.

Sneha added, perfectly calm:
"By the way, why didn't **you** cover it?"

Even the baby smirked.

The Afternoon She Collapsed

One chaotic afternoon:

- Maid absent
- Plumber demanding entry
- Delivery guy asking for OTP
- Washing machine beeping like a judgmental auntie
- Baby screaming
- Dal burning

- Pump battery dying
- Her back cracking

Sneha sank onto the sofa and whispered,
"I can't do this."

The invisible load doesn't break you significantly.
It breaks you like a hairline crack in glass—
quietly, slowly, until suddenly everything shatters.

The Reset

That night, Sneha took a notepad.
And wrote everything she did.

It filled **two full pages.**

She gave it to Rohan.

He read it.
His face changed.
He looked like a minister who finally read the budget he approved.

"You do ALL this?" he whispered.

Sneha nodded.
"And I'm tired."

Rohan swallowed.
"Tell me what I can take over."

She circled three tasks:

- Groceries
- Paediatric appointments
- Evening bath time

"Groceries? Cool, I'll order. Appointments? Okay. Bath time? No chance — you handle that, I'm genuinely scared I'll drop him."

And feeling oddly proud of this tiny contribution, he wandered back to the TV, fully convinced he'd helped in a big way.

The First 10% Shift

It wasn't magic.
It wasn't fifty-fifty.
It wasn't intense.

But it was something.

Rohan did order groceries — sometimes on his own, mostly after Sneha reminded him and Alexa joined the follow-up committee.

He booked the vaccination appointment without drama, which felt like genuine progress.

And he even gave the baby a bath once… after Sneha practically dragged him in. He held the baby like a ticking bomb, ready to explode at the slightest splash

And for the first time since childbirth, Sneha felt…

Not free.
Not rested.
Not transformed.

But **lighter.**

Not because the work vanished—
but because she wasn't carrying it alone,
at least not anymore. Rohan had finally started pitching in…
even if half of it was because Sneha stood over him like **a supervisor on probation.**
She exhaled.

What she didn't know was that this tiny 10% shift
would spark a bigger question lurking in the shadows:

If he can take some load…
can I take some of my life back?

A question waiting to explode in the next chapter.

CHAPTER 5 — MARRIAGE AFTER BABY

(Or, How Two Adults Can Live Together, Love Each Other, Have a Baby… and Still Misunderstand Everything)

Before the baby, Sneha and Rohan had a simple, sweet rhythm.

Two humans.
One Wi-Fi.
One Netflix account.
One bed (unshared blanket, but shared warmth).
Dinner.
Snuggling.
Bitching about bosses.
Occasional fights about coriander in noodles.
Laundromat dates.
Weekend plans.
Random cuddles.
Inside jokes.
A soft, lovely "us."

Then the baby arrived.

And marriage after baby felt like a **group project where one person was doing a PhD and the other had just learned how to highlight text in Google Docs.**

Sneha once believed marriages broke because of "communication problems."

Now she knew the truth:

Marriages struggle because both partners are living the same crisis… from completely different planets.

Sneha's Planet:
Feed. Burp. Cry. Rock. Diaper. Repeat.
Laundry. Bottles. Pumping.
Leaking nipples.
Molten back pain.
Three hours of sleep across twelve hours.
Running a household like a crisis call-centre.

Rohan's Planet:
Office. Traffic. Coffee.
WhatsApp.
Lunch break.
Office gossip.
Maybe gym.
Reels.
Return home.
Expect applause for "being responsible."

Same house.
Two universes.
Zero overlap.
Infinite misunderstandings.

Marriage Math That Doesn't Add Up"

BEFORE BABY:

Sneha: 50% of household
Rohan: 50% of household
Total: Partnership ✓

AFTER BABY:

Sneha: 95% of baby + 70% household + 80% of emotional labour = 245%
Rohan: 50% of income + 5% of baby + 10% "helping" = 65%
Total: Doing 400% work

THE PROBLEM: The math is broken.
THE SOLUTION: Recalculate. Redistribute. Renegotiate.

The 1:13 A.M. Fight That Was Never About Sleep

It was 1:13 a.m.
The baby was screaming like he was filing an HR complaint.

Sneha got up, ribs shaking from exhaustion.

Rohan rolled over like a man adjusting the AC in a resort.

"Sneha… please," he mumbled.
"Chup karao yaar, I need to sleep. I have office tomorrow."

Sneha blinked at him as if witnessing an alien species.
"Office tomorrow?" she whispered.

"Yeah… big meeting…"

Something prehistoric rose inside her —
a beast created from sleepless nights, leaking breasts, pumping trauma, and feminist rage.

"I ALSO have work tomorrow."

"You're on maternity leave," he muttered.

"Maternity. LEAVE."

Even the baby paused — sensing an incoming volcanic eruption.

"Maternity leave is NOT a vacation, Rohan.
It's not Goa.
It's not a spa.
It's WORK.
My boss screams every hour. INTO MY EARDRUMS."

The baby wailed again, just to emphasise.

Rohan sat up, offended.
"Arre, I'm ALSO tired! You think earning is easy?"

Sneha didn't scream.
She went quiet.

The dangerous kind of quiet.
This wasn't about sleep.
Or diapers.
Or chores.

It was about one sentence she had been aching to say:

"I am drowning.
And you don't even know there's water."

The Missing Husband

Sneha didn't miss sex.
Or dinner dates.
Or fancy outings.

She missed her partner.

The man who held her hand while grocery shopping.
The man who asked, "How's your heart?"
The man who listened.

Now their conversations were transactional:
"He pooped."
"Where's the diaper?"
"Did you sterilise the bottle?"
"Why is he crying?"
"Where are my socks?"

The tenderness evaporated.
The softness evaporated.

Sometimes even **the WE** evaporated.
They had become co-workers.
in a crisis-management start-up
neither had applied for.

The Kitchen Collapse

One afternoon, after six chores, four meltdowns, three leaks (various sources), and one burnt roti, Sneha stood at the sink holding a feeding bottle and simply… stopped.

Her brain whispered:
I can't do this.
I'm disappearing.
I'm becoming useful… but invisible.

Rohan walked in, saw her expression, and panicked like a man spotting a cockroach.

"What happened? Are you okay?"
Sneha looked up — eyes hollow, voice thin.

"I need my partner back."

Not anger.
Not blame.
Just truth.

Rohan's instinctive defensiveness rose… but something in her face made it drop back down.

He saw her —
really saw her —
for the first time in weeks.

"Tired.
Lonely.
Frayed.
Still fighting."

His voice softened.
"Okay."

A tiny moment.
But the beginning of change.

The Awkward, Sweet Attempt at Reconnection

That night Rohan patted the sofa like a man offering VIP seats at a seminar titled "*How Not to Be a Clueless Husband 101"*.

"Come sit," he said.

Sneha sat.
Cautious.

Rohan poured her water in his filmi style.
"Aapka paani, madam."

She snorted.

They talked — awkward, aimless, familiar.
Old holidays.
Traffic.
Stupid office gossip.

It felt like flat soda — no fizz but still strangely comforting.

Then the baby farted loudly.

They burst into laughter.
Their first real laugh in weeks.

For a moment, something warm flickered.

Later, Sneha leaned her head on Rohan's shoulder.
Not sexually.
Emotionally.

He misread completely.

He lowered his voice, Zee TV drama-style.
"Wanna… do something?"

Sneha recoiled like she'd touched a live wire.

"ROHAN. No. NO.
I leaned for EMOTIONAL SUPPORT.
My nipples hurt.
My stitches hurt.
I stink.
I haven't slept since Independence Day.
And YOU want item-song romance?!"

Rohan raised both hands like he was negotiating a hostage situation.

"Sorry! Sorry! I didn't know! I thought you were... in the mood!"

"In the mood? In THIS milk-stained T-shirt?! In THIS postpartum jungle?!"

They whispered-argued.
Honestly.
Clumsily.
Tenderly.

And finally, Rohan whispered the first truly honest thing he'd said in weeks:

"I don't know how to read you anymore.
I'm scared I'll do the wrong thing."

Sneha's anger melted — just a little.

"I don't know how to read myself either.
But I need you to learn WITH me.
Not guess."

No kissing.
No swelling music.
No instant resolution.

But something shifted.

Understanding.
Just a flicker.

And flickers can light up entire rooms.

Tiny Attempts. Big Shifts.

The next week, Rohan tried.

Not perfectly.
Not grandly.
But sincerely.

He took one night feed.
He sterilised bottles (wrongly the first time, but with great enthusiasm).
He held the baby while Sneha showered.
He sat next to her when she cried and just… stayed.

Sneha noticed.
Not because he became perfect —
but because he became present.

They still snapped at each other.
Still misunderstood each other.
Still fumbled between exhaustion and intimacy.

But the walls lowered.

The team feeling resurfaced —

tentatively, shyly, like a plant growing after a storm.

The 3 A.M. Moment That Changed Everything

At 3:00 a.m., the baby cried.

Sneha instinctively moved to get up.

But Rohan placed a gentle hand on her arm.

"I'll go," he whispered.

"You?" she asked, genuinely surprised.

He nodded.

He walked to the crib like a man walking into a battlefield.
He rocked the baby.
He hummed something off-key — somewhere between a bhajan and a broken ringtone.
And somehow… it worked.
Ten minutes later he returned with the baby asleep on his chest.

Sneha watched them.
And something inside her softened.

Hope.

Not fairy-tale hope.
Not "all problems solved" hope.

Just quiet, tired, human hope:

We're learning.
We're trying.
We're not alone in this anymore.

Sneha closed her eyes.

For the first time in weeks,
she slept a little deeper.
A little steadier.
A little safer.

Because motherhood hadn't changed.
Marriage hadn't magically healed.
Life hadn't become easier.

But she was no longer carrying it alone.

And that — finally — was enough.

CHAPTER 6 — THE BREAKING POINT

(Or, how a Mother Can Hold It All Together… Until One Text Message Makes Her Shatter)

There comes a moment in every new mother's life when she breaks.

Not theatrically.
Not Karan Johar movie-style running in the rain.
Not with violins or slow motion.

Just quietly.
Privately.
Devastatingly.

Sneha's breaking point arrived on the most ordinary Thursday afternoon.
The kind of day no one remembers —
except she would, for the rest of her life.

Her oversized nursing gown featured an abstract, milk-stained map of India.
Her bun had retired from holding hair and was now held together by two mismatched clips and sheer hope.
Her chai — reheated thrice — sat on the table, cold and betrayed.

A single baby sock lay on the floor, mocking her.
Babies, for reasons known only to the gods, remove exactly one sock at a time, like it's part of their union agreement.

Sneha had slept **forty-one minutes** the previous night.
Her body ached as if her bones were held together by Fevicol.
Her eyelids stung.
Her back felt forged in a pressure cooker.
Her knees trembled.
Her patience dangled by a thread thinner than postpartum hair.

Then everything happened at once.

The washing machine beeped like a judgmental auntie.
The cooker whistled like an angry Delhi landlord.
The baby wailed like he had been personally betrayed by life.
The doorbell rang.
Her phone buzzed.

It buzzed with a message from Rohan:

"Lunch bana? Dinner mein kya hai?"

Four words.

Four innocent, culturally conditioned, wife-to-mother-to-house-manager words.

That detonated every nerve in her spine.

Sneha stared at the phone.
Then at the ceiling fan spinning uselessly.
Then at nothing at all.

Her brain whispered:

"I am done."

The Motherhood Meltdown

At **3:42 p.m.,** Sneha sank to the floor.

Not with an audience.
Not as a cry for attention.

She simply didn't have the energy to remain upright.

She placed the baby beside her, gently, on a blanket — the only gentleness she had left — and let her head fall into her hands.

And she cried.

Not pretty tears.
Not slow, cinematic Madhuri tears.
Not the elegant "one tear drop" heroines are allowed.

These were blotchy, messy, runny-nose, chest-shaking tears. The tears of a woman who had been holding an entire universe together with nothing but breast pads and willpower.

She cried because she was tired.
She cried because she felt invisible.

She cried because she didn't recognise herself.
She cried because motherhood consumed her like a forest fire.
She cried because asking for help felt like failure.
She cried because needing help felt even worse.
She cried because the guilt was eating her alive.

But above all —
she cried because she missed being **Sneha.**

Not Mumma.
Not the milk machine.
Not the diaper expert.
Not the default parent.
Not the emotional shock absorber.
Not the walking-talking to-do list.

Just Sneha.

The girl she once was.

The baby stared at her.

Then, in one tiny, perfect gesture of human tenderness, he reached out and placed his little palm on her cheek.

Sneha laughed through her tears —
the hysterical laugh of a woman too tired to choose a single emotion.

Rohan Walks into A Storm He Didn't See Coming

At 6 p.m., Rohan walked in.

He saw the unwashed dishes.
He saw toys scattered like evidence of a crime scene.
He saw the baby cranky and half-asleep.
He saw Sneha's swollen, red eyes.

And instead of asking "Are you okay?",
instead of holding her,
instead of reading the room,

he asked:

"You didn't cook?"

Sneha looked up.

Her eyes weren't angry.
They were hollow — empty, resigned, drained of performance.

She stood.
Walked up to him.

"I cried for an hour," she said quietly.

Rohan blinked.
"Why?"

Sneha's voice came out flat — the voice of a woman who had crossed the emotional event horizon.

"Because I'm exhausted, Rohan.
I'm going under.
I'm doing everything alone.
And the only thing you're worried about… is food."

Rohan puffed up immediately.
The male defensive stance from ancient patriarchy activated.

"I WORK all day too! You think office is a picnic? You think I do NOTHING? You think—"

"STOP."

Sneha's voice cracked through the room like thunder.

The baby startled awake and began crying — because babies have impeccable showmanship timing.

Sneha picked him up, shaking, breath uneven.

"This is NOT about you, Rohan," she said.
"Not everything is about you.
For once, just LISTEN."

Rohan froze.

This wasn't the moody Sneha he thought he understood.
This wasn't hormones.

This wasn't "overreacting."

This was a woman who had reached the edge of her humanity.

The Fight That Finally Said the Truth

Sneha placed the baby down gently.
Her hands trembled.

"Do you know how many hours I sleep? Two. Maybe three. My back hurts. My head buzzes. My nipples hurt. My stitches hurt.
My emotions are hanging by dental floss."

Her voice cracked.

"I haven't eaten a full meal in weeks.
My body isn't mine.
My time isn't mine.
My mind isn't mine."

She pointed to his text.
"And you're asking me 'lunch bana?'"

Rohan opened his mouth — ready to argue again — but she raised her hand sharply.

"No.
You speak ONLY after you listen."

Rohan shut his mouth.

And finally —
finally —
he looked at her.

Not at her messy hair.
Not at the unwashed dishes.
Not at the baby crying.
Not at the clothes everywhere.

At her.

The woman who had held their universe together while he assumed she was "managing."

He saw the cracks.
He saw the exhaustion.
He saw the cost.

And something inside him shifted.
A small shift.
But real.

The Soft Collapse

Rohan stepped forward.
Carefully.
Like approaching a wounded bird, he desperately wanted to protect but didn't know how.

"Sneha…" he whispered.

She didn't look up.

Gently, he placed his hand on her arm.

"I didn't know," he said.
"I honestly didn't see it."

Sneha let out a painful, broken laugh – the kind that wasn't really a laugh at all.

"Exactly.
You didn't see.
Because you've never **had** to."

She looked at him then – eye swollen, voice trembling but steady.

"And Rohan…I know you're trying. I do. But buying cute online gifts for the baby and cracking those lame 'lighten the mood' jokes – it's not helping. It's actually irritating me.

Because in all this chaos, your casual 'How's your day?' or 'Lunch bana?' might sound normal to you… but Rohan, *I'm not the same person anymore."*

Her voice broke, softer now, almost a whisper.
"Where am I in all this?
How am I?"
Who am I turning into?
Have you asked me ever once?"

She wiped a tear with the back of her hand.

"I'm changing every day. I don't even understand what's triggering me half the time…I don't know who I'm becoming. I'm just…trying to hold on."

His throat tightened.
He had no defence left – only the truth settling heavily between them.

"I'm sorry," he said.

Two small words.
Not magical.
Not grand.
Not a fix.

But true.

And Sneha didn't forgive instantly.
She wasn't a Bollywood heroine in a chiffon saree reconciling in the rain.

But the wall lowered – just a sliver.

And in marriage, sometimes that sliver is the miracle.

The Night Everything Clicked

That night, Rohan didn't touch his phone.

Didn't open Netflix.
Didn't pretend to be tired.

He took the baby – awkwardly, clumsily, earnestly.

He changed the diaper.
He rocked him.
He hummed a lullaby so off-tune even Alexa would reject it.
Rohan panicked but didn't quit.

Sneha watched from the bed – eyes red, body aching, soul tired – but comforted.

For the first time, she wasn't the only one standing in the fire.

At one point Rohan looked at her, eyes wide:

"How do you do this every day?"

Sneha whispered,
"Because I have no choice."

Rohan's expression cracked – guilt, empathy, awakening blending together.

He held the baby closer.

And in that moment,
Sneha felt something she hadn't felt in months:

Not joy.
Not relief.
Not magic.

But something quieter.
Deeper.
Truer.

She wasn't alone anymore.

Not saved.
Not healed.
Not fixed.

But no longer alone.

And sometimes, that is enough.

CHAPTER 7—
POSTPARTUM RAGE & THE SILENT VOLCANO

(Or, How One Wet Towel Can Trigger Ten Generations of Feminist Fury)

Nobody warns women about postpartum rage.

Not doctors.
Not aunties.
Not relatives who otherwise have advice on everything from burping to breathing to picking the "right" dal for lactation.

Why?

Because postpartum rage doesn't fit the glow-up, "divine motherhood," cotton-kurta, peaceful-aarti image society likes to photocopy onto women.

Imagine a parenting book saying:

"Congratulations! You may feel like throwing a steel spoon at your husband."

Not great marketing.

So, Sneha discovered postpartum rage the way most women do:
accidentally, explosively, and over something stupid.

---

1. The Shoe Trip +Baby Chaos

It started with Rohan's shoes.

Those two leather landmines.

Always in the wrong place.
Always underfoot.
Always mocking her.

Sneha walked out of the bedroom, baby on her hip, and **tripped** over the same pair for the 97th time in 40 days.

She stumbled forward—
BONK!
The baby's rattle flew into her forehead like a weapon thrown by a tiny, untrained ninja.

And then it hit her—
not the rattle, the **rage.**

A sudden blast furnace in her chest.

Hot.
Immediate.
Violent.
Shocking.
Sneha froze.

"What is wrong with me?" she whispered.

She wasn't sad.

She wasn't irritated.
She was angry – raw, hot, full-bodied anger.

And it scared her.

---

2. Where Did This Anger Come From?

She sat down on the floor, heart racing.

This wasn't about shoes.
Or socks.
Or the rattle that just tried to murder her.

It was:

- sleep deprivation
- body pain
- overstimulation
- nonstop responsibility
- invisible load
- constant touch
- zero silence
- hormonal chaos
- being needed every minute
- being judged every hour
- and the deep injustice of motherhood changing her life 500% while Rohan's changed maybe 12% (on a good day).

This wasn't madness.

This was **overwhelm. This was her nervous system filing an HR complaint against life.**

---

3. Flashback – Her Mother's Silent Rage

Sneha remembered a scene from childhood:

Her mother, standing in the kitchen at 11 p.m., scrubbing a pan aggressively while the rest of the house slept.

Her father snoring.
Her brother playing video games.
Sneha doing homework.

Her mother's eyes were red.
Her jaw tight.
Her movements sharp.

She wasn't shouting.
But Sneha felt the storm.

Mothers weren't allowed to explode.
So, they imploded.

Sneha suddenly realised:

She wasn't the first woman to feel this rage.
She came from a lineage of woman trained to smile through it.

Generation after generation women to feel this rage.
She came from a lineage of women trained to smile through it.

Generation after generation women who held the universe together but never held space for their own emotions.

---

4. The Mother-In-Law Trigger

The next day, MIL arrived and noticed Sneha's tense shoulders.

"Beta, you look irritated," she said.
"Motherhood requires patience. Baby senses everything."

Translation: **Your emotions are wrong.**

Sneha felt the volcano expand inside her.

But she swallowed it.

Like generations of women before her.

---

5. The Legendary Wet Towel Incident

Every Indian marriage has a "Wet Towel Moment."

Sneha's arrived at 7:45 a.m.

Baby screaming.

Breakfast burning.
Her back cracking.
Her bra strap snapping.

She entered the bedroom.

There it lay—
The wet towel.
Majestic.
Sprawled.
Leaking onto the bedsheet like an uninvited guest who refuses to leave.

Sneha stared.
The towel stared back.

Something snapped.

"HOW MANY TIMES, ROHAN!?
AM I THE CLEANING STAFF HERE!??
WHY IS THIS TOWEL HERE AGAIN!?"

Rohan froze mid-brushing, toothpaste foam at the corner of his mouth, looking like a man who had just witnessed a woman being possessed.

"Sorry?" he squeaked.

"SORRY?! YOU HAVE ONE JOB!"

Her voice echoed.

And then, immediately, guilt washed over her.

Why was she screaming?
Why couldn't she control herself?
What was happening to her?

She didn't know yet.
But she would.

Because towel fights are never about towels. They're about everything except towels.

---

6. The Pressure Cooker Phase

Over the next few days, Sneha didn't shout.

She swallowed.

swallowed irritation.
swallowed frustration.
swallowed unfairness.
swallowed noise.
swallowed expectations.

She became a walking pressure cooker—
whistle missing, steam rising, danger imminent.

The world tells women: "Don't get angry."
The world tells mothers: "You must be patient."

But no one asks:

"Who is patient with the mother?"

---

7. The Chips-In-Bed Eruption (The Climax)

It was 9 p.m.
The baby had finally slept after Olympic-level rocking.

Sneha sat on the sofa, breathing trying to feel human.

Rohan sat next to her…and casually opened a packet of chips.

Inside their **bed.**

Crunch.
Crunch.
Crumbs falling like confetti.
Crumbs sticking to the bedsheet.
Crumbs entering Sneha's soul.

And something inside her snapped.

"ARE YOU KIDDING ME, ROHAN!?
CHIPS IN BED!?
CHIPS!?
IN BED!?

Rohan looked up, stunned.
"Arre, it's just crumbs—"

"IT'S NOT THE CRUMBS!

IT'S EVERYTHING!
I'M CARRYING EVERYTHING!
I'M RUNNING ON EMPTY!
AND YOU'RE DROPPING CRUMBS!"

The baby began crying (babies know exactly when to contribute to drama).

Rohan finally said softly—
"I thought you were angry at me…"

Sneha shouted, crying at the same time:

"I'M ANGRY BECAUSE I'M OVERWHELMED!"

And for the first time,
Rohan's face softened with understanding.

"Oh," he whispered.

A small word.
But in marriage, small words can shift worlds.

---

8. The First Time Sneha Asked for Help.

It didn't happen after a big fight.
Or a dramatic breakdown.
Or someone sitting her down and saying, "*You need help.*"

It happened on an ordinary night.

The house was quiet.
The baby had finally fallen asleep.
Her husband was snoring softly, unaware.

Sneha was awake.

Crying without sound – the way mothers learn to cry.

Not because one thing was wrong.
But because **everything felt tangled,** and she couldn't find the end of the thread anymore.

She wasn't sad exactly.
She wasn't angry either.

She just felt…stuck.
Like she had reached a dead end inside her own head.

That night, she didn't Google diagnoses.
She didn't read articles.

She just thought:

I need someone to help me untangle my thoughts.
Someone who isn't family.
Someone who isn't expecting me to be strong.

The Decision

A few days later, on an afternoon when her husband had gone to office, Sneha asked her help to come with her.

Sneha hadn't told anyone where she was going. In her world therapy still felt like a whispered word— something you say the way people said "constipation" at family dinners.

She didn't explain much.
Didn't dramatize it.

Just said,
"Come with me. I need to talk to someone."

The baby came too.
The maid waited outside.

Life didn't stop to accommodate her pain – and she didn't expect it to.

The Room

At her session, Sneha finally allowed the words to escape.

"I feel guilty," she said.
"I feel out of control."

The therapist smiled gently – the kind of smile that didn't judge, didn't diagnose, didn't say "yeh sab normal hai, beta."

"Sneha, postpartum rage isn't bad behaviour," she said softly.
"It's a **signal.**"

"A signal?"

"Your needs aren't being met.
Your boundaries are unclear.
Your support is insufficient.
Your emotional bandwidth is EMPTY.
Rage isn't the problem.
It's the message."

Sneha's throat tightened. She felt tears rise. Her eyes burnt.

"I'm not… crazy, rt?"

"No," the therapist said, steady and kind.
"You're overwhelmed.
BIG difference."

And in that quiet room – the one she entered with shame and reluctance – Sneha finally felt something she hadn't felt in months:

Seen.
Understood.
Human.
It wasn't forced.
But it was a turning point.

The kind Hindi TV serials never show –
the scene where the heroine stops pretending, she's fine…and starts returning to herself.

For the first time in months, Sneha felt seen.

What Changed

She didn't walk out healed.
Nothing magical happened.

But something shifted.

She felt **lighter,** not because her problems disappeared –
But because they were finally spoken aloud.

- ***NOTE FOR READERS***
- ***A Small Note, If You're Wondering***
- *Seeing a counsellor doesn't mean something is wrong with you.*
- *Sometimes it simply means:*
- *your thoughts have become too loud*
- *you're tired of explaining yourself*
- *you need a space where no one needs anything from you*
- *In India, we're taught to "adjust," "manage," and "be strong."*
  We're rarely taught what to do when our mind feels full.
- *Talking to a counsellor is not giving up.*
  It's pausing long enough to breathe — so you can keep going.
- *You don't need permission.*
  You don't need a label.
  You don't even need to tell anyone, until you're ready.
- *Asking for help is not weakness.*
  It's a quiet form of courage.

---

9. Cooling The Volcano

Sneha started tiny changes:

- Saying "I need help"
- Giving Rohan specific tasks
- Taking micro-breaks (even 3 minutes)
- Naming her feelings instead of swallowing them
- Letting herself feel anger without shame

She wasn't becoming perfect.

She was becoming **honest.**

---

10. Rohan Steps Up

Rohan began noticing triggers:

- Shoes → moved
- Wet towel → hung
- Crumbs → avoided
- Baby duty → volunteered
- Emotional cues → registered
- Sneha's silence → understood

Not perfectly.
But sincerely.

And sincerity was enough.

---

11. Slow Softening

One evening, Sneha rocked the baby peacefully.
He placed his tiny hand on her chest and giggled.

She smiled.

The volcano was still there.
But it wasn't erupting.
It wasn't swallowing her.

She wasn't broken.
She wasn't crazy.
She wasn't failing.

She was a woman carrying too much –
And finally, slowly, sharing the load.

The volcano wasn't her identity.

It was just her signal.

And now?
She was finally listening to herself.

✨ **Bonus: Sneha's 60- Second Reset for Angry Moms**

1. **Stop. Put baby down safely.**
2. **Touch something cold (fridge door/ steel glass)**
3. **Inhale for 4 counts.**

4. **Hold for 4.**
5. **Exhale for 6.**
6. **Name the feeling: "I'm overwhelmed, not angry."**
7. **Ask for help. Immediately.**

You deserve support.
Not strength.
Support.

CHAPTER 8—
THE MYTH OF HAVING IT ALL
(Or, How Sneha finally Stopped Competing with Instagram and Started Competing with Herself)

Sneha grew up believing a lie.
A beautifully packaged, capitalism- sponsored lie:

"You can have it all."

The perfect marriage.
The perfect body.
The perfect baby.
The perfect skin.
The perfect job.
The perfect house.
The perfect glow.

The perfect everything, simultaneously, without a single hair out of place.

Basically, the Buy-1-Get-10 Combo Pack of Modern Womanhood.

Now that she was a mother, Sneha finally understood:

This was the **greatest scam** ever sold – bigger than fairness creams, ICSE Maths, and missing Tupperware lids.

And the place that sold this lie the most?

INSTAGRAM.

The Scroll That Ruined Her Day

It was a regular Sunday.
Sneha sat on the floor in an overworn T-shirt that smelled faintly of baby drool, spilled chai, and the last 14 days of her emotional exhaustion.

The baby was throwing toys like a one-man IPL team warming up.

A rattle hit her foot.
A plastic cup rolled away.
Something sticky— mango or sadness – decorated the sofa.

Sneha opened Instagram.

Mistake.
Fatal mistake.

The first reel:
A mom in silk pyjamas, hair in soft waves, baby sleeping peacefully on her chest.
She glowed. She sparkled. She radiated serenity.

Caption:
A rattle hit her foot.
A plastic cup rolled away.

Something sticky— mango or sadness— decorated the sofa.

Sneha opened Instagram.

Mistake.
Fatal mistake.

The first reel:
A mom in silk pyjamas, hair in soft waves, baby sleeping peacefully on her chest.
She glowed. She sparkled. She radiated serenity.

Caption:
✨ *Balancing motherhood and success… feeling blessed.* ✨
#MomBoss #EffortlessLiving #GlowGoals

Sneha looked at her own reflection on the black TV screen.

She was glowing too—
from sweat, milk leaks and possibly suppressed tears.

The Comparison Spiral

Reel 2: A Pilates mom using her toddler as a kettlebell.
Reel 3: A mom painting in a spotless living room. Not a single stain. Not a single fingerprint. Impossible.
Reel 4: Snack-brand-launching mompreneur.
Reel 5: A fashion influencer mom with perfect hair and a cooperating child.

Sneha muttered,
"Cooperating baby? Which species in that?"

Her own baby hurled a spoon full of massed potato at the wall. Within minutes, Sneha slipped into the comparison Olympics.
It was like lays packet – once you start, you don't stop.

Them: glowing
Her: **sweating**
Them: thriving
Her: **surviving**
Them: finishing 10k runs
Her: **finishing finding the remote under the sofa.**
Them: Launching businesses.
Her: **launching yet another the washing machine cycle**
Them: organic smoothies
Her: **reheating chai for the fourth time.**

She wasn't jealous.
Fine, she absolutely was.

But mostly…she felt she was failing.

The Elevator Truth— Reality Arrives Wearing Cotton Kurtas

Later that evening, Sneha ran into Tara from the 8th floor—the Instagram queen whose feed looked like the ZARA Home mood board.

Sneha braced herself.

But Tara sighed and said,
"Thank God you asked how I'm doing. I'm barely surviving. Today's post? Old photo. Today my toddler painted my ALL the walls. I cried in the bathroom."

Sneha blinked.
"Wait… that reel wasn't from today?"

Tara laughed.
"Are you mad? No one posts reality. NEVER. Reality is chaos."

Sneha stepped out of the lift lighter.
A little less alone.
A little less fooled.

The Journal Breakdown

That night, Sneha opened her journal and wrote everything she believed a woman was "supposed" to do:

Healthy meals
Tummy time
Child development activities
House clean
Career intact
Glow maintained
Patience unlimited
Sexy wife

Fit body
Spiritual morning routine
Happy baby
Happy husband
Happy in-laws
Happy Instagram feed

Halfway through, she burst into laughter.
Then tears.
Then laughter again.

"How is ONE woman supposed to do ALL this?"
Answer: She isn't.
But society expects her to.

No one ever tells fathers to "have it all."
Only mothers are handed this invisible syllabus of the impossible.

The problem wasn't her life.
The problem was the expectations. And that's the truth no one says out loud.

The Mall Meltdown— The Recovery Edition

At the mall, the baby refused to latch.
Sneha's hands shook.
Tears threatened.

Then a stranger— a woman with soft eyes – entered.

She placed a hand on Sneha's shoulder.

"Breathe. You're doing good, Mumma."

HER.
She was doing good.

The baby calmed.
Sneha calmed.
A tiny crack in the myth appeared.

The Food Court Fight (Featuring French Fries and Male Cluelessness) – First Real Boundary

Sneha returned to the food court.

Rohan, happily eating fries, asked:
"All okay? Why so long?"

Sneha stared.

He wasn't rude.
He wasn't malicious.
He was simply… unaware.

For him, it was "long."
For her, it was 40 minutes of silent labour + emotional labour + nipple trauma.

Instead of exploding, she simply said, "Next time, you feed him,"

And Rohan blinked.
Then nodded.

A small moment.
A huge shift.

Baby Milestone→ Mother Milestone

That evening at home, the baby suddenly pushed forward.

Then again.

Then again.

He crawled— Not beautifully— Not gracefully— but like a drunk squirrel discovering ambition.

Sneha froze.
Her heart flipped.
The baby shrieked in victory.
Sneha laughed—
the first real, belly-deep laugh in months.

If HE can move forward… maybe I can too.

The 3 Things Mothers Can Drop Without Guilt

At the end of the day, Sneha wrote three truths in her journal:

1. **The need to be perfect.**
2. **The pressure to do everything.**
3. **The habit of comparing her life to curated reels.**

Her therapist's words echoed:
"Comparison kills joy. Reality builds resilience."

Sneha closed her eyes, breathing softer.

She didn't have it all.

But she had enough.
And that was everything she needed.

CHAPTER 9—
THE CALENDAR THAT CHANGED EVERYTHING

(Or, How One Red Circle Took Down an Entire Week of Peace)

The Calendar Attack— and Sneha's First Calm Reaction

Sneha was having a golden week— a rare, mystical, unicorn-like phenomenon in early motherhood.

The baby slept four hours.
Twice.
Rohan handled bedtime without consulting YouTube.
Sneha showered.
Alone.
She even drank chai hot, which felt like winning a Padma Shri.

For the first time since giving birth, Sneha thought:

"Maybe…MAYBE…I'm finally getting the hang of this."

And then she saw the calendar.

The red circle.
The date she had once marked confidently.
Her maternity leaves end date— TWO WEEKS away

Her heart dropped like a lift with faulty wiring for a moment.

Then…she inhaled.
Held the wall for support.
And asked herself a question she hadn't asked in months:

"Sneha, what do You want?"

Flashback: The Women She used to Be

Sneha closed her eyes and saw her old Office self:

Walking with Purpose.
Her mind sharp.
Desk Plant thriving.
Excel Sheets and Name on emails that mattered.

Shipping terrible machine Coffee like it was a personality.

She missed that rhythm.
That competence.
That version of herself who wasn't constantly covered in milk, exhaustion and expectations.

Now she couldn't remember the last adult conversation she had that wasn't about burping or diapers.

The contrast felt like a slap from her old life.

The Work-Wardrobe Humiliation

Sneha opened her wardrobe with great optimism
BUT—

Her old trousers mocked her.
Her blouse buttons applied harassment complaint.
Her zip refused resurrection.

Sneha stared at her reflection:

"I look like a potato wearing another potato," she whispered.

As if summoned by her insecurity and destiny, the TV blared:

"New mom actress spotted looking FAB just 8 weeks after delivery!"

a glowing celebrity stepping out of the gym with visible abs, hair blowing like it had its own PR team.

Sneha froze; a sharp current ran down her spine like lightening.

"8 WEEKS?! I still walk like my bum is on fire."

Another reel auto played:
A fitness influencer mom saying,
"Ladies, you can bounce back easily! Just stay consistent!"

Sneha grabbed her postpartum belly flap and muttered, "Hummm…, consistency. I'm consistently leaking milk."

She switched the TV off aggressively— as if she was defending all postpartum bodies from impossible standards.

Her body wasn't something she hated—
it was something she was **still living inside,** healing inside, learning inside.

But everywhere she looked, women seemed to "bounce back"
while she was still trying to bounce out of bed.

Rohan Walks into An Emotional Landmine

Just then, Rohan entered the room carrying two cups of chai like he was applying for Best Husband (in the Quarterly review).

He saw her staring at the calendar.
"Oh," he said, "Your office…two weeks."

Sneha nodded silently.
"You'll manage, na? You always do."

It was meant as encouragement.

It detonated her brain.

She forced a smile, but inside she was screaming.

"I Don't Want To Manage Anything Anymore."

The Family Circus of Unsolicited Advice

Somehow, news spread.

MIL: "Office abhi rehne do. Baby Chhota hai."
FIL: "Job is important… but baby is more important."
Mom: "Do what you want…but beta, this time and age never returns."
Brother: "Don't lose career momentum."
Cousin: "Hire a nanny."
Neighbour aunty: "Six-month baby in daycare? Hai Hai."
Society: "whatever you choose, YOU are wrong."

Sneha wanted to scream: **"Can someone give me ONE correct answer?!"**

The Monologue that Finally Freed Her

She snapped.

"If I stay home— I'm wasting my degree.
If I go to work— I'm a selfish mother.
If daycare— I'm cruel.
If nanny— irresponsible.
If I'm tired— I'm weak.
If I look fine— I'm still not enough.
If I do ONE thing for myself— it's too much."

Tears spilled. Then the real truth burst out:

**"And NOT ONCE has anyone asked me:
Sneha, what do YOU want?"**

It wasn't meltdown.
It was a breakthrough.

Rohan froze like Wi-Fi in the rain.

She Finally Says It Out Loud

"I don't think I'm ready to go back," she whispered.

Rohan sighed.
"But EMIs…plans…we agreed—"

She raised her hand.

"I'm not asking for permission.
I'm telling you where I am mentally."
It wasn't rebellion.
It was honesty. It was clarity.

Rohan Tries to Help (In his UPSC Way)

That night, Rohan sat on the bed secretly Googling like he was preparing for civil services:

"How to support wife going back to work."
"Signs of maternal burnout"
"Safe compliments postpartum."

One said: *"Be supportive."*
He nodded.

Another said: *"Ask what she needs."*
He underlined this mentally.

Another said: *"Buy her chocolate."*
He closed the tab. Too risky.

Then he came to her and said simply.
"Tell me what's going on inside you."

It wasn't perfect.

But it was partnership.

The Therapist's One-Liner That Cut Through the Noise

The next day, Sneha told her therapist everything.

Her therapist listened and said one line Sneha needed:

"Motherhood brings choice fatigue— because every choice feels life-defining.
So, choose the one that keeps you whole."

Sneha inhaled slowly, something shifted.

Her First True Choice Since Becoming a Mother

That night, Sneha sat with a notebook.
She wrote:

Pros
Cons
Fears
Desires
Her mental bandwidth
Her physical energy
Her emotional readiness

And finally:

"What choice keeps me whole?"

The answer rose quietly inside her:

She needed more time.
She wasn't ready.
Not yet.

For the first time, the decision wasn't guilt- driven.
Not fear-driven.
Not society- driven.

It was **her.**

The Baby Makes The Decision Clearer.

Later, as she held the baby, his tiny fingers curled around hers – soft, trusting, anchoring.

He sighed and fell asleep on her chest.

And Sneha felt her decision settle peacefully in her bones.

She whispered,
"We'll figure this out, you and me."

And she meant it.
The Air Changes.

At bedtime, she told Rohan:

"I'm taking a sabbatical."

He paused. Looked at her and then nodded.
"If that's your choice…I'm with you."

She exhaled deeply—
for the first time in months.

She wasn't "managing."
She wasn't just "coping."
She wasn't losing herself.

She was choosing herself.

And that changed everything.

Sneha Didn't "Have it All." But She Finally Had Herself.

She wasn't perfect.
Wasn't glowing.
Wasn't sorted.
Didn't have an organic routine or a colour-coded calendar.

But she had clarity.
She had courage.
She had herself.

And for the first time since giving birth… that was enough.

CHAPTER 10—
THE DAY SNEHA FINALLY ASKED FOR REAL HELP

(Or, how a Pressure Cooker Lid Became the Catalyst for a New Marriage)

It happened on a Sunday.

Officially Holiday for Men.
Unofficial Overload Day for Women.

Rohan lay on the sofa scrolling reels.
The baby threw carrot sticks with the confidence of a cricket bowler.
Maid absent.
Laundry mutinous.
Lunch was half-burnt.
And Sneha stood holding the pressure cooker lid like a discus thrower considering her options.

Then Rohan asked a sentence so dangerous, even goddesses flinch:

"Lunch mein kya hai?"

Sneha didn't shout.
She froze.

Every husband should fear THIS level of calm.

The Breakthrough

Sneha inhaled. Exhaled. And said, softly.

"Rohan, I need help."

"Humm? Yeah, sure.", he said, still scrolling.

She placed the pressure-cooker lid down *too gently*—
the before-tsunami signal.

"No, Rohan. Not 'help-wala help."
Not occasional help.
Not when-you-feel-like-its help.

REAL help.
Consistent.
Shared.
Without reminders.
Help I don't have to beg for.
Help I don't feel guilty asking for."

His phone lowered in slow-motion..

"I cannot run this house alone.
I can't be the default parent.
I can't be the emotional shock absorber for everyone.
I am NOT the only adult here."

Her voice was calm, steady, undeniable.

"I NEED PARTNERSHIP."

Rohan stared at her, seeing the woman behind the exhaustion.

"What needs to change?" he finally asked.

Operation: Marriage Reset

Sneha outlined the new plan with CEO clarity.

"1. Evening baby duty— one hour.
Daily. No excuses."

Nod.

"2. Groceries— your responsibility."

Nod.

"3. Sterilizing bottles— yours."

Swallow. Nod.

"4. Weekend laundry— definitely yours."

Slow nod.

"And Sunday morning?
My time. Alone. Non-negotiable."

Rohan took a breath— "Done."

The Radical Thing Sneha Did

She didn't say,
"Are you sure?"
"Is that okay?"
"Thank you SO much!"

For the first time, Sneha didn't minimise, apologise, or sugarcoat. She simply said:

"Good. I need this."

No apology.
No guilt.
Just truth.

Sneha had officially entered her **Boundaries Era.**

The First Trial Run— Chaos + Comedy

At 6 p.m., Rohan took the baby for his one-hour duty.

Within 12 minutes:

- He dropped the rattle
- Wiped banana off baby
- Then wiped banana off himself
- Burped the baby incorrectly

- Got peed on
- Lost the pacifier
- Found the pacifier in his shoe
- Panicked
- Sweated
- Questioned all his life choices

The baby screamed in his ear in Dolby Atmos.

Rohan felt the cry vibrate through his skull.

It wasn't normal sound.
It was spiritual torture.

It felt like someone had rung **a church bell inside his head.**

He staggered into the living room, hair standing up, eyes wild, like a man returning from War.

"How…do…you…DO THIS…every day?".

Sneha sipped her chai— actual **hot chai—** Smiled:

"Exactly."

Rohan's Meltdown Call

Later, on call with his friend Arjun from the balcony, he whispered into his phone.

"Arjun… bhai… lag gayi.
He cried nonstop for FORTY minutes straight.
My brain melted.
My head is still vibrating."

Arjun laughed.
Rohan did NOT.

He went on, "I think my back is broken.
He screamed when I put him DOWN,
He screamed when I picked him UP,
He screamed when I breathed. His scream was so loud that even a sperm whale would've felt underqualified."

Arjun, "So Sneha does this all day?"

Rohan, "All day. Every day.
And I… I had no idea.

I thought earning was the hard part.
Turns out… I had no idea."

For the first time, he wasn't just helping.
He was understanding.

Sunday Morning— Her First Real Break

Sneha woke up early that day.

Not because the baby cried.
Because **she had time.**

HER time.

She went to a café. Sat alone.
Ordered one hot chai and bun maska.

The first sip tasted like freedom.
For ten whole minutes, Sneha wasn't holding a baby,
a bottle, or responsibility.

She was holding **herself— something she hadn't done in months.**

Breaking The Motherhood Curse

While sitting there, Sneha thought of her mother—
the woman who never asked for help,
never rested,
never took a break.

Sneha felt a warmth in her chest.

Her mother survived motherhood. Sneha wanted to live it.
She smiled.

She wasn't failing.
She was rewriting the script.

A Quiet Golden Night

That night, after Rohan's second day of baby duty (and he survived), they sat together quietly.

He said,
"Thank you…for telling me you were drowning."

Sneha replied,
"Thank you… for listening."

"And I'll keep listening," he said.
"And I'll keep telling you,"she smiled.

No loud Bollywood Music.
No bid declarations.
Just two tired humans… finally on the same team.

She wasn't fighting for air anymore.

She was rising—
one boundary, one hour of partnership, one guilt free hot chai at a time.

CHAPTER 11
THE FIRST GLIMPSES OF HERSELF AGAIN

(Or, The Week Sneha Realised She Was as Still in There Somewhere)

The day Sneha sent the email, her hands shook.

She had rewritten it **thirty-seven times.**

One version was too emotional.
One was too formal.
One sounded like she was applying for leave to go to Goa.
One sounded like she was resigning forever.
One simply said: "HELP"

She deleted that one.

Finally, she wrote:

Subject: Request for Sabbatical Extension
Hi Ma'am,
I would like to extend my maternity break into a short sabbatical due to health and caregiving needs.
I hope the team can manage without me for a few more months.
Thank you for your understanding.
-Sneha

Her finger hovered over "Send."
Her heart thudded.

She clicked it.

Immediate regret.
Then relief.

Then sadness.
Then scare.
Then… calmness she hadn't felt in months.

The Office Replies – Imperfectly Perfect

An hour later, her manager replied:

**"Hi Sneha,
Take the time you need. Your well-being matters.
We'll manage internally till then.
Don't worry.
Warmly,
Meera."**

Sneha took a breath of relief.
Feeling held. Warm. Kind. Human.

Five minutes later, HR replied:

"Noted.

Please fill form-17A, attach medical certificates, update on portal, and schedule compliance call."

Sneha blinked.

This was the emotional equivalent of:

"We bless your journey." + "Fill this form in triplicate."

She felt an odd mix of:

- Relief
- Grief
- Detachment

- Pride
- Fear
- Unexpected freedom

She realised something:

The office was a world she had given so much to…and it kept moving, without her, without hesitation.

And maybe, just maybe, that was ok.

The Week of Small Wins

The next few days felt different.

Lighter. Warmer.

The baby slept a little better.
Rohan took over evening duty without reminders.
Sneha drank chai without rushing.
She read a full article – in one sitting, without someone throwing up on her.

Her brain, once mushy like upma, was slowly re-solidifying.

She felt tiny sparks of "Old Sneha" Return – not fully but glowing faintly.

The Salon Tragedy of 2024

Sneha decided she deserved a hair wash.

Not a haircut.
Not a blow – dry.

Just a simple hair wash – the minimum form of self – respect.

The hairdresser ran her fingers through Sneha's hair…

…and came away holding what looked like raw material for a wig factory.

"Hawww! Hair fall is too much! Ma'am, stress?"

Sneha stared at her blankly, thinking:

"No, I'm just in motherhood. Every hair is resigning voluntarily."

As the hairdresser massaged oil into her scalp, clumps fell like autumn leaves.

Sneha almost cried.
Almost.

Then she laughed.
Because honestly, what else CAN you do when your hair is submitting resignation letters in batches?

She left the salon smelling like jasmine, feeling lighter in the head and oddly tender—
as if someone had tidied a small corner of her life.

The Mom Friend She Didn't Know She Needed

At the paediatrician's clinic, Sneha met another mom – Riya.

Riya was breastfeeding with the confidence of someone who had given up on modesty weeks ago.

They bonded instantly over:

- Cracked nipples
- Burp anxiety
- Husbands
- Supermom-ism
- Clingy phases
- Why babies only poop on fresh clothes

"Let's walk together tomorrow?" Riya suggested.

Sneha nodded.

For the first time in ages, Sneha wanted the plan.

The Mini Fight That Didn't Become a War

That evening, Rohan forgot to warm the bottle.

Sneha snapped:
"Rohan! I told you—"

Then stopped.

He looked genuinely apologetic.

Not defensive.
Not irritated.
Just human.

"I'm sorry," he said quietly, "I'm learning. I'll do better."

And Sneha…exhaled.

"No, I'm sorry too. We're both tired."

They hugged in the kitchen –
awkward but warm, real and gentle.

Not cinematic. And real was better. It was healing.

The Walk That Wasn't Just a Walk

The next morning, Sneha actually got out. Stroller, water bottle, diaper bag, mild hope – all loaded.

Riya was already downstairs, rocking her stroller like a pro who had negotiated peace treaties with colic.

They started walking around the complex.
Slow Steps.
Uneven Sleep.
Matched Pace.

No Agenda.
No Pressure.

Two tired mothers trying to remember how sunlight felt.

"I still can't believe we're out," Sneha said.

Riya laughed. "Honestly? Same."

They walked past the security guard, who gave the universal nod of respect reserved for mothers managing strollers and sanity at the same time.

For a few minutes, they spoke about usual things – feeds, diapers, husbands, night shifts, unsolicited advice –
the script all new moms know by heart.

Then, halfway around the park, Riya's voice softened.

"You know…she wasn't easy to get," she said, nodding toward her sleeping baby.

Sneha looked at her, confused.

Riya exhaled – that long tired, practiced exhale of someone used to holding stories alone.

"We tried for years," she said quietly.
"Four rounds of IVF."

Sneha stayed silent.
The wind suddenly felt colder.

"The injections…" Riya paused.
"God, the injections broke me. The hormones…the mood swings…the weight gain…the way my body didn't feel like mine."

She wiped a tear before it slipped.

"And then after she came, everyone only sees the miracle. Nobody sees what it cost me to bring her here."

Sneha felt something tighten in her chest.
She hadn't expected this.
She hadn't expected her – this confident, funny, open Riya – to be carrying something so heavy.

Riya continued, softer now:

"I love her. Of course I love her.
But every time someone calls me 'lucky', I want to scream.
Lucky?
I fought for her.
I bled for her.

I stabbed myself with needles every night for her."

Sneha looked at her—really looked—at the dark circles, the stretch marks peeking under her T-shirt, the tired smile that carried more hurt than anyone would guess.

"I didn't know…" Sneha whispered.

"How would you?" Riya said.
"We don't tell each other these things. We just survive them alone."

The babies slept.
The world moved.
Two mothers stood on a footpath, sharing pain that had no audience.

And in that moment, something shifted in Sneha.

She realised:

It's not easy for anyone.
Not the mothers who conceive easily.
Not the mothers who fight for years.
Not the mothers who adopt.
Not the mothers who miscarry.
Not the mothers who breastfeed.
Not the mothers who don't.
Every woman is carrying a story.
Every mother is holding a heartbreak.

Every journey has its own battle scars.

And all this time, Sneha had thought she was alone.

But walking next to Riya – stroller wheels squeaking, bodies tired, hearts cracked open – she understood:

None of us are doing this alone.
We just haven't been saying it out loud.

Sneha's Mother – The Conversation That Healed Something

One afternoon, Sneha video-called her mom.

"I took a sabbatical," she confessed.

Her mother paused.
Then smiled softly.

"Good," she said.
"You're choosing yourself.
I never did.
I didn't know how."

Sneha's throat tightened.

Her mother continued:

"You're doing what I couldn't, beta.
You're building a new way for your family.
I'm proud of you."

Sneha closed her eyes, letting those words stitch something inside her that had been torn since childbirth.

Maybe generational healing doesn't happen in big moments.

Maybe it happens in sentences like this.

The Baby's Perfectly Timed Milestone

That evening on the playmat, the baby looked at her…paused.
And gave his FIRST big, gummy, beautiful laugh.

A real laugh.
A from-the-belly laugh.

Sneha gasped.

He laughed like he'd discovered joy for the first time – and maybe she was discovering it again too.
In that moment, she felt:

rewarded,
seen,
chosen,
healed.

Not because motherhood got easier—But because she finally was experiencing it from a place of strength, not exhaustion.

Mirror, Mirror—She's back Moment

Later, while brushing her thinning hair, Sneha caught her reflection.

Tired.
A little frizzy.
A little drained.

But her eyes?

They looked clearer.
Calmer

More…like her.

"I'm coming back," she whispered.

Not the old Sneha. Not the pre-baby Sneha.

A new Version of her—
wiser, softer, stronger, and finally…whole.

Her journey was changing.

And so was she.

CHAPTER 12—
WHEN LIFE FOUND ITS RHYTHM…AND THEN THE BABY STARTED CRAWLING

(Or, How Sneha Thought She Was Back in Control Until Her Son Turned into a Mini Parkour Athlete)

Sneha had entered a strange new stage of motherhood—something between survival and semi-stability.

Not peace.
Not balance.
But she **wasn't fighting for air anymore.**

She was…floating.

Chai wasn't always cold.
Showers happened without existential tears.
She had gone two whole days without snapping at Rohan.
Progress, not perfection – but progress.

But the biggest sign?

Sneha no longer woke up crying at 4 a.m.

Now she woke up at 6:48 a.m.
To Rohan still snoring beside her like a wildlife documentary voiceover.

Somethings never change.

Sneha tiptoed out, reheated yesterday's chai (Round 1 of many), and mentally listed the day's tasks.

And then — crawling happened.

The Day Crawling Arrived Uninvited

One second, the baby was on the playmat, drooling peacefully.
The next second – missing.
Sneha's soul briefly left her body.

He reappeared under the sofa, grinning like a thief in training.

And then, life became a chase sequence.

The baby crawled like:

- a Swiggy delivery boy on a deadline
- a Squirrel after Red Bull
- a Puppy discovering turbo mode
- Drunk Friend at a sangeet trying to find a balance

He went everywhere – under tables, behind curtains, towards slippers, into the bathroom (door left open by Rohan, obviously).

Sneha aged 11 years in four days.

Rohan: Trying, But Only When Being Asked

When Rohan finally woke up 37 minutes later, scratching his head and adjusting his T-shirt, she said:

"Baby's crawling."

He blinked. "Like…crawling crawling?"

"Yes, Rohan. Not metaphorically."

He jumped into action instantly – but badly.

He tried to 'help', which mostly meant:

- Following the baby around like a confused shadow
- Kept asking, "Should I pick him?" every 2 minutes
- Let the baby chew on his headphone wire
- Panicked: when baby moved fast ("Is this NORMAL speed?!")

He was chaotic beyond doubts. But he tried.
And Sneha noticed.

The Effort.

Effort felt like romantic song now.

The Famous Baby Gate Incident

Rohan installed the baby gate.

Upside down.

The baby crawled under it within 40 seconds, giggling like he'd outsmarted a national security system.

Sneha laughed so hard, she had hiccups.
And Rohan, being Rohan, blamed the instruction manual as usual.

Somethings never change and probably should not either.

The Mini-Bump and the Big Realisation

One afternoon, the baby bumped his cheek lightly on the sofa edge and started wailing.

Baby screamed.
Rohan panicked.

"SNEHHAAA! He hit his FACE! He's HURT! Can't you take care of him? Should we go to the Hospital?"

Sneha calmly picked the baby up, checked him, kissed his cheek, and soothed him.

"You're okay, babu."

Rohan stared at her like she was a Zen master.
She wasn't always calm esp. after motherhood. But today she was.
"You're so calm", Rohan whispered.

Sneha realised…she was. **Therapy had quietly rewired something in her – she didn't freeze, didn't panic, didn't react, just…responded.**

And she felt proud.

The Honest Self-Talk

That night, washing bottles, Sneha had one of those small, honest internal conversations.

"Sneha…you don't have to hold the whole universe together alone."

Another thought followed:

"The world didn't collapse when she rested.

The office didn't collapse without her.
The house won't collapse if chores wait."

She wasn't enlightened.
She wasn't transformed – but she was learning to breathe again.

Some days were still disasters.
Some evenings still cracked her open.
Some nights she cried in the bathroom.

But she was learning to breathe again.
Her Updated Survival Notes

She scribbled in her notebook:

Rule #7: I don't need to do everything at expert-level.
Rule #8: Trying is still trying, even if it's clumsy
Rule #9: Rohan needs instructions—not telepathy.

She underlined Rule #9 thrice.

The Sideways Step

That evening, the baby stood up holding the sofa and took one sideways "cruise" step— unsteady, messy, wobbly.

Sneha gasped.

Rohan cheered like India won the World Cup.
The baby squealed noticeably.

Sneha felt emotional too.

Not because her son was learning to stand.

But because she was, too…
Wobbly, Messy, Imperfect. But rising.

CHAPTER 13—
THE TODDLER PREVIEW (9-12 Months of Recurring Chaos)

(Or, How Sneha Finally Found Her Balance…and Then Lost It Again Daily)

By the time the baby was around nine months old, something shifted—in the home, in Sneha, in the marriage.

The panic faded.
The breathlessness eased.

Sneha woke up one morning, looked at her sleeping child, stretched her back (carefully, always carefully), and realised:

"I am not fighting for air."

She wasn't floating, exactly.
But she was swimming.
Badly, awkwardly, with one arm, maybe— but swimming, nonetheless.

The house had found a rhythm:
a messy, unpredictable, inconsistent—
but a rhythm.

And that felt like winning.

The Baby's Personality Arrives…Loudly

Around this age, babies stop being potatoes and start being people.

Sneha's child became a full-blown character.

He had:

- opinions
- moods
- preferences
- drama
- mischief
- toddler-level chaos energy…as if he got Duracell fitted in him.

He hated caps.
He refused green peas like a freedom fighter.
Threw tantrums as the ball rolled away from him.
He laughed for ten straight minutes at the fridge magnets like they were stand-up comedians.

And then he discovered – the Brahmastra – **fake crying.**

Oh, the drama.

If Sneha walked out of the room:

WAAAAAAHHHNNNNNNN—

Pause.
Peek.
Check if she was watching.
If yes → resume performance.
If no → stop crying and inspect remote control.

Sneha couldn't decide whether to applaud or groan.

Rohan whispered, "He's exactly like you."

She threw a pillow at him.

Rohan Tries Being a Fun Dad

New dads develop a deep desire to teach their babies the most useless things.

Rohan had started teaching him:

- growling
- clapping theatrically
- "ta-da" poses with both hands raised
- eyebrows wiggling
- how to make "Buuu…rrrrr….aaahhhh…" sound, until baby's face is full of drool

"Why are you turning him into a tiny Tollywood villain?" Sneha asked.

Rohan puffed up. "He likes it!"

The baby growled happily.

Sneha sighed.
But secretly, her heart melted at the ridiculous duo she called hers and enjoyed looking at them.

The First "Baby with Daddy" Long Shift—A Shaky Success

One day, Sneha decided she needed a real haircut.

A real one.

Not the "trim-two-strands-and-run-back-home" haircut.

"Are you okay alone with him for a couple of hours?" she asked.

"Of course!" Rohan declared confidently.

Sneha raised an eyebrow.
He swallowed.
But he managed.

Two hours later, Sneha returned to find:

- the baby alive
- the house not on fire
- Rohan exhausted but proud.
- and banana mashed into the curtain, which she chose not to mention.

Sneha realised something important.

She didn't HAVE ***to be the only parent.*** Relief washed over her.

The Deepest Self-Talk – Her Quiet Awakening

On that quiet night, when the house was finally quiet, Sneha stood by the window, staring at the city lights.

A strange clarity rose inside her—the kind that comes only after months of surviving, fighting, breaking, healing, rising.

She whispered to herself:

**"Sneha…it's not everyone else.
It's you."**

Not blame.

Not criticism.
Truth.

"You gave yourself too much importance…
too much pressure…
too much responsibility…
as if everything falls apart without you."

A breath
Deep
Steady

"But nothing fell apart.
Your office ran smoothly.
Your team moved on.
Life didn't stop.
The world didn't break when you stepped back."

She touched the glass, watching the reflection of a woman she almost didn't recognise for months.

"You don't have to do it all.
You don't have to hold everything.
You're not the engine of the universe.
You're just…you.
And that's enough."

She felt the weight loosen off her shoulders—the weight she had placed there herself.

Mom Survival Notes – New Entry

In her little notebook, she wrote:

"I am not scared of motherhood anymore."

And for the first time, she truly meant it.

The Baby's Next big Milestone – And Sneha's Too

One evening, while Sneha and Rohan sat on the floor sipping chai.

The baby stood next to the sofa holding it…
balanced…
looked at them with pure mischief…
…and took **one tiny sideways step…**

Sneha gasped.
Rohan cheered.
The baby squealed, proud as a peacock.

Sneha's eyes filled.

Not because the baby took a step.

But because **she had too…**

A step out of fear.
A step away from guilt.
A step towards herself.

He was learning to stand.
And so was she.

The house glowed with laughter, chai warmth and soft evening light.
Sneha inhaled deeply.

Life wasn't perfect.
Life wasn't calm.
Life wasn't sorted.

But it was hers.

And for the first time in a very long time…
she loved it.

CHAPTER 14— THE QUIET TRANSFORMATION

(Or, The Day Sneha Realised Growth Doesn't Arrive with Fireworks)

It happened on a random morning.

No enlightenment.
No violin soundtrack.
No cinematic glow up.

Just Sneha, awake before everyone else, sitting with warm chai (finally warm), listening to the city hum.

Rohan was still asleep, snoring gently.
The baby was babbling at the ceiling fan.
The house was messy but calm.

And for the first time in months…
Sneha didn't feel like she was gasping for breath.

Not healed.
Not glowing.
Not the "back to normal" everyone talks about.

But lighter.
Clearer.
More Herself.

The Subtle Changes

She noticed herself doing things differently:

- pausing instead of snapping
- asking for help without guilt
- letting go of perfection

- choosing rest over martyrdom
- not spiralling at every comment

Not always—
but often enough to matter.

Some days still broke her.
Some afternoons still exploded.
Some nights still left her exhausted.

Healing wasn't linear.
She was healing, nevertheless.

The Accidental Meditation (Thanks To Baby)

Sneha opened YouTube to watch a recipe of her favourite Chef – Ranveer Brar.
But before Ranveer could say in his affable line – "Aur aap kahenge ki Ranveer aapne bataya nai", the baby slapped the screen.

Sach mein…(Ran)Veer aapne bataya nai

Suddenly a guided meditation began.

She almost changed it.

But her shoulders ached.
Her heart felt heavy.
Her mind needed…something.
She let it play.

For the first time in months, her mind sat still.
Like a toddler finally napping after hours of chaos.

And a quiet thought rose inside her.

"Maybe I'm not supposed to go back to who I was. Maybe I'm becoming someone new."

Someone softer.
Someone calmer.
Someone who belonged to herself again.

Her Mother's Words – Soft, Unexpected and Needed

Later that day, her mother watched her for a moment and said:

"You've changed, beta.
Not in a bad way.
In a stronger way."

Sneha's throat tightened.

Her mother wasn't one to give compliments. But this one landed softly—like a tiny bandage on a year-long wound.

The Apology She Owed Herself

That night, Sneha stood before the mirror.

She didn't see stretch marks or tired eyes or the softness of her belly.

She saw a woman who had carried a baby,
a household,
and generations of expectations.

She whispered:

"I'm sorry."

For pushing herself too hard.
For expecting perfection.
For living to please others.
For shrinking herself for peace.

Then she added, ever so gently:

"Thank You for Surviving."

It wasn't melodramatic.
Just honest.

The Unapologetic Shift

Sneha realised something else:

She was done living for others.
Done apologising.
Done shrinking.
Done being the "good girl."

Motherhood had broken her open —
but through the cracks, light had entered.

She wanted to live unapologetically now.
Not aggressively.
Not rebelliously.
Just truthfully.

Some days she would succeed.
Some days she wouldn't.

But the shift had begun.

For real.

Ending – Her Balcony Moment

Later that night, she stood on the balcony, breathing in the cool air.

The baby slept.
The house was finally quiet.
Rohan murmured in his sleep, dreaming who-knows-what.

Sneha whispered:

"I'm not the old me.
I'm not my mother's version of me.
I'm becoming my own version."

She wasn't a perfect mother.

But she was finally becoming a whole woman.

And—quietly, slowly, beautifully – that felt enough.

CHAPTER 15 —
THE MOTHERHOOD TIME MACHINE (THEN VS NOW)

(Or, Why Sneha's Mom Had More Hands but Fewer Choices)

It started with a sound.

Not a profound one.
Not a baby giggle.
Not a wise old woman chanting mantras.

It was…
her mother laughing.

Her mom was visiting for the weekend and had taken the baby to the balcony.
Sneha heard the baby squeal, her mother giggle, and a faint, nostalgic tune – some old 90s song about rain and heartbreak.

Sneha watched them from the doorway and thought:

"How the hell did she do this with THREE kids?"

Her mother spotted her and said,
"Arre, in our time, babies were easier."

Sneha raised an eyebrow.
Babies? Easier?

Or…
Either the 80's children came with factory-installed sleep settings,
or memory loss was a government-approved postpartum benefit.

THEN: The Joint Family Manufacturing Setup

Sneha's mother explained:

"In our time, beta…
there were people everywhere around.
Aunty, chachi, neighbour, bhabhi, cousin, vegetable-wala, random child who lived next door…"

Basically, parenting in those days looked like:

1 mother → 10 babysitters
1 crying session → 6 aunties commenting
1 meal → cooked by 3 women
1 tantrum → handled by collective Indian motherhood DNA
1 sick child → entire mohalla offering remedies
1 mother → rarely left alone

Kids were practically raised between courtyard cricket and kitchen gossip.
Sneha pictured it like a desi Amazon warehouse:

Efficient. Crowded. Loud. Free delivery of unsolicited advice.

NOW: The Nuclear Family Hunger Games

Sneha mentally compared her reality:

Her version of motherhood:

- No courtyard
- No balcony big enough for even one plastic chair
- No extended family
- No neighbour dropping by

- No relatives within 70 km
- No joint kitchen
- No random cousins entertaining the baby
- No group supervision
- No aunties physically assisting (only judging via WhatsApp)

Her support system:

- Rohan (trying, rebooting regularly),
- Her parents and in-laws (sometimes),
- Riya (one screaming child of her own),
- Her Househelp (the backbone of India),
- and Amazon Prime same-day delivery,
- Google
- And so on…

Earlier mothers had villages. Modern mother's village is Wi-Fi.

Earlier mothers had people.
Now mothers have search engines.

And Yet…Her Mom Had It Hard Too

Sneha watched her mom hold the baby on her hip like muscle memory from 1992…humming softly, and realised:

Her mother wasn't pampered.
She wasn't supported emotionally.
She wasn't thanked.
She wasn't acknowledged.

She had:

- help
- hands

- a community

But she did NOT have:

- respect
- autonomy
- emotional support
- rest
- appreciation
- validation
- permission to say, “I’m tired.”
- the freedom to choose HERSELF.

Sneha whispered under her breath:

“Different battles. Same exhaustion.”

The Little – Little Supports They Had (And We Lost)

Her mom told stories of:

- neighbours dropping hot food
- aunties holding crying babies
- women cooking together
- someone always sitting with mom during breastfeeding
- older cousins distracting toddlers
- washing dishes and gossiping
- sabudana khichdi magically appearing without being ordered

Compare that to now:

Today, Sneha would be LUCKY if the neighbour smiles before closing her door.

Modern motherhood is lonely.
Even in high-rise buildings filled with families.

A Moment Of Gratitude (And Grief)

In the kitchen, her mom chopped vegetables while holding the baby on her hip like it was nothing.

Sneha watched in awe.

Her mother said,
"In our time, nobody asked how the mother was. We only talked about the baby."
Sneha quietly replied,
"In my time, nobody is around to ask."

There it was.

Two Generations.
Two Wounds.
Two Truths.

Earlier:
Tons of Hands, Zero acknowledgement.

Now:
Tons of acknowledgement online, zero help in real life.

The Emotional Punchline

Sneha realised:

Her mother's generation was tired.
Her generation was tired and *alone.*

Her mother's generation had hands.
Her generation had self-help books.

Her mother's generation had community.
Her generation had Google.

Her mother's generation had loud houses.
Her generation had quiet apartments.

Her mother didn't get appreciation.
Sneha didn't get support.

Both deserved better. Both lacked something essential.

And suddenly Sneha understood:

She wasn't weak.
She was operating without safety nets that existed for centuries.

She was doing a job meant for a village – inside a 2BHK – with a baby who thought slippers were snacks.

A Warm, Funny Moment

That night, her mother told her:

"You're doing very well, beta."

Sneha grinned.
"Of Course, Ma, I am raising *this shaitaanu* without the 14 women you had."

Her mother swatted her arm playfully.

"You're raising him with Amazon and Google. That's 14 people only, if not More."

They laughed –
A shared laughter of two women
From two different eras
realising motherhood changed

But love hadn't.

She went to bed knowing:

She wasn't failing. She wasn't slow.

And she was doing the job brilliantly.

CHAPTER 16 – THE VILLAGE SNEHA BUILT FROM SCRATCH

(Or, How Sneha Collected People Like Life Jackets Without Realising It)

Motherhood, Sneha had learned the hard way, was not meant for one woman.
It was a job designed for tribes, clans, communities, nosy aunties, nosier neighbours, cousins, grandmothers, and the entire human population of a mid-sized Indian town.

Her mother had a village.
Her grandmother had a village.
Even pre-historic cavewoman had a village.

Sneha had…
Amazon | Google | Zepto | Swiggy
And the Society guard who sometimes smiled at the baby.

But somewhere between sleepless nights, crawling chaos, Rohan-learning-reboot updates and emotional breakthroughs, Sneha realised something surprising:

She had built a village.
Quietly. Slowly. Accidentally.
One human at a time.

Not the loud, coconut-oil smelling joint-family village of old India.

A Modern Village.

A DIY, crowdsourced, urban, slightly dysfunctional, surprisingly strong village.

A village made of mismatched pieces – like one of her baby's wooden puzzles.

THE MOM FRIEND: RIYA – Her Emergency Contact for Sanity

Sneha didn't exactly know when she and Riya became so close.

One moment they were politely nodding in the paediatrician's waiting room,
the next moment they were WhatsApping voice notes that began with:

"Tell me I'm not a bad mother because today I fed him Marie biscuits for lunch."

Riya had become Sneha's **Postpartum SOS Helpdesk.**

They traded:

- trips
- recipes
- complaints
- screenshots of questionable Google searches
- and confessions like
  "Sometimes I pretend I can't hear him cry so my husband picks him up."

They weren't just friends.
Modern moms aren't friends – they are survival partners.

Riya wasn't family.
But she was village.

THE STRANGER WHO SAID THE MAGIC LINE

Sneha still remembered that day in the mall – milk-stained, exhausted, hands shaking in the nursing room.

The baby refused to latch.

Her breath quickened.
Her eyes burned.

Then a woman knocked softly and said the most needed line in all of motherhood:

"You're doing good, Mumma."

Sneha never saw her again.

Sometimes a village doesn't stay.
Sometimes it appears just long enough to stitch a woman back into herself.

HER MOTHER – A New Kind Of Support

Sneha saw her mother differently now.

Not an authority.
Not a critic.
Not the keeper of "how mothers should behave."

But a woman –
doing her best with the tools and restrictions of her time.

Her mom didn't live nearby.
Didn't understand modern gadgets.
("Why banana feeder? Just give banana, na.")

But when she came?

She brought presence.
Warmth.
A lap that had raised three kids.
Wisdom disguised as casual dialogue:

"Let him cry a little, beta. His lungs are strong."

Her mother wasn't the whole village anymore.

But she was a wiser, gentler part of it.

THE THERAPIST— Emotional First Aid

Sneha had walked into therapy thinking she was "just tired".

She walked out realising she had been burning on low flame for months.

The therapist didn't talk about burping, naps, or weaning.

She handed Sneha something bigger:

Clarity.
Language.
Perspective.
And Permission.

Permission to be human.
Permission to not be perfect.
Permission to ask for help.
Permission to rest without guilt.

Therapy wasn't part of her mother's village.

But it was probably essential to hers.

THE MAID – The Underrated MVP

Sneha finally admitted to herself:

Without the Unofficial Board Member aka maid, she would have evaporated into fine dust particles.
This woman, who came in smelling of Ponds powder and wielding a mop like a weapon, had saved Sneha's sanity more times than she could count.

She didn't give lectures.
She didn't judge.

She simply said:

"Didi, aap baitho. Main kar deti hoon."
With the calm assurance of a superhero lifting a bus.

Modern Indian motherhood would collapse without women like her.

This wasn't "help".
This was structural support.

She, too, was village.

THE WHATSAPP MOM GROUP (Chaotic but Comforting)

Sneha had joined the "Moms of Orchid Residency" group out of boredom.

She stayed because it reminded her, she wasn't alone.

At any hour,

Someone was awake.
Someone was venting.
Someone was asking - "Is green poop normal?"
Someone was sharing discounts.
Someone was sending memes about husbands not understanding diaper rash.

It was messy, noisy, overwhelming – like a virtual mohalla.

But Sneha felt held.
Digitally, but genuinely.

This was the **new-age courtyard.**

And Then, There Was ROHAN

The newest, freshest addition to the village.

Not perfect.
Not instinctive.
Sometimes confused.
Sometimes stagey.
Often late on tasks.

But trying.
Present.
Learning.
Evolving.

Sneha realised she wasn't "lucky" he was helping – she was finally getting what she deserved:
A partner, not a supervisor.

His efforts – fumbling, awkward, sometimes upside-down baby gates—
were another brick in her support system.

This, too, was village.

The Big Realisation

One evening, while watching the baby crawl toward the balcony door, Sneha whispered to herself:

"I didn't have the village my mother had…
But I didn't raise this baby alone."

She listed her village:

- Riya
- the Stranger
- her mother
- the maid
- the therapist
- the moms group
- Rohan
- even herself – the strongest pillar
- and the baby, who unknowingly pushed her to grow

This wasn't the old-style village system.
Not built on geography or duty.
It was built on heart.
Choice.
Connection.
Shared struggle.
Shared humour.
Shared survival.

A modern village.
But still a village.

The Line That Ties It All Together

That night, Sneha opened her journal and wrote:

**"It didn't take a village to raise my child.
It took a village to raise me."**

Because motherhood, she now understood, was never about who held the baby.
It was about who held **her.**

And for the first time in her journey,
Sneha didn't just feel supported.

She felt **belonging.**

CHAPTER 17 —
THE SOFT REVOLUTION

(Or, The Year Rohan Finally Noticed the Sink)

Nobody warned Sneha that motherhood didn't just create a baby –
It quietly, slowly, painfully, hilariously created a new husband.

Not a perfect one.
Not a modern Instagram husband with folded laundry and almond-milk smoothies.
Just…Rohan 2.0

Still glitchy.
Still loading.
But updated enough to notice the difference.

The Team Bonding Fiasco

Rohan forgot on a Thursday.

Not forever.
But just long enough to hurt.

"I'll be home by nine", he said that morning, kissing my forehead while I stirred oats with one hand and held the baby with the other.

"Okay". She replied.
But what She meant was—
"Please don't be late. I am already operating at my limit."

At nine, Sneha texted:
"On the way?"

At ten,
"How long? Baby's been crying for a while".

At 11:45, the door finally opened, Rohan walked in smiling, phone in one hand, laughing.

"How was your day?", he asked casually. "We had drinks after so long, Rahul was so hilarious today…"

Sneha was sitting on the floor.
The baby was asleep on her chest after four straight hours of teething screams. Her kurta was soaked, the house wrecked.
Sneha replied, controlling – "I've been along with a screaming baby for fourteen hours".

"Oh", he said, "Was it that bad today?"

"Bad?", Sneha repeated. "He's teething Rohan, he screamed for almost four-five hours."

"Well…these things happen", Rohan replied defensively. "It was an office get together, Team Bonding. You know how it works; I couldn't just leave. I'm earning, someone has to."

That sentence.

The one we'd already dissected. The one which hurt. The one he knew was wrong.

Sneha stood up slowly, looked at him once, and said, "Goodnight."

She slowly walked to the room with their son in her arms closed the door and locked it.

In the morning, when Sneha got up, Rohan was near the door, sitting on the floor.
"I fucked up", he said immediately. "I said the exact thing I had promised, I wouldn't."
Then he said something, that mattered.
"My father said that to my mother, my uncle ji to aunty ji almost everyone all the time said in any argument– "I'm working. I am earning to take care of everyone needs" … And we absorbed it, like it was the truth."
Rohan looked at Sneha carefully,
"I don't want to become Him. And I don't want you to disappear like my mother did".

Sneha replied, quietly but firmly, "This is your warning. Not because I want to threaten you. But because I won't keep teaching you how to see me."

Sneha stood up. Held her hand out.
"Come on, baby's about to wake up. And I need chai."

.

Something shifted in Rohan. He learned that sometimes you **need to unlearn** to make things better. He stopped assuming.
We stopped absorbing. We both became aware.
And that is how change actually begins –
Not with grand gestures,
But with awareness, the only way forward.

The Breakfast Incident

The first sign of evolution arrived on a sleepy Saturday morning.

Sneha woke up expecting chaos.
Instead, she found Rohan in the kitchen wearing the expression of a man performing brain surgery.

He had made breakfast.

If you could call it that.

One plate of soggy oats.
One slice of toast burnt at the edges.
A banana cut very unevenly.
And a cup of tea that tasted like determination.

He stood proudly like he was MasterChef's guest judge.

"Look!", he said, "I made everything".

Sneha smiled.
Not because the breakfast was good.
It wasn't.
But because the effort was adorable.

Progress, not perfection.

The Plate-In-Sink Achievement

Rohan then placed his plate in the sink.

Like an adult.
Like a responsible man.
Like a national hero.

And then… he waited.

After a long pause, he finally said,
"I kept my plate in the sink."

Sneha, without looking up:
"Okay."

Rohan:
"No, I mean…by myself."

Sneha smiled and patted his back.
"Shabash"

And just like that, a feminist revolution happened…
very slowly…
very splendidly…
inside a 2BHK in Goregaon.

The Dish-Washing Hero (Maid On Leave Edition)

The next week, the maid didn't show up.

Sneha braced herself.

But Rohan walked to the sink like a martyr heading into a battle.

After ten minutes of furious scrubbing and heavy sighing loud enough to shake the ceiling fan, he emerged victorious.

"All done", he announced, "Whole Sink. Alone. Without help."

Sneha blinked.

He looked exhausted.
Sweaty.
Traumatised.
She said softly,
"Congratulations."

He nodded proudly.
This was his Everest.

The Swiggy Solution

Another day, the maid was late.

Without missing a beat, Rohan said:

"Let's order from outside today. No need to struggle."

Sneha blinked.
This was the most practical sentence he'd said in months.

They ordered Biryani.
It was delicious.
They didn't even pretend to feel guilty.

The Realistic Fight (The One All Couples Have)

That evening, Rohan flopped on the sofa with a sigh loud enough to scare pigeons.

"Sneha", he said dramatically,
"It was such an exhausting day. Sometimes I feel like you don't SEE how much I do."

Sneha stared.

Rohan sat up, emotional engine revving:

"I'm trying SO hard. I've changed so much! I do office all day AND help at home. *Papa kabhi kitchen mein nai gaye the.* But you don't appreciate it."

Ah yes – the Indian husbands' "Why Don't You Clap for Me?" anthem.
Sneha inhaled deeply.
Her therapy training activated.

"Rohan…I do appreciate you", she said gently, "Truly. But parenting isn't 'helping'.
It's your job too."

He frowned, defensive.

Sneha gently added,
"And I'm tired too. Just because I stay quiet doesn't mean I'm not exhausted."

Rohan's shoulders dropped.
His expression softened, but only a little.

He wasn't "fixed".
He was listening.

And that was enough for now.

The Baby-Care Evolution (Still Loading)

Rohan took over feeding one evening.

He proudly wiped the baby's face afterward.

Except…

rice still on forehead
carrot in eyebrows
dal in one ear
yogurt on chin.

He presented the baby like a finished painting.

"Clean!"

Sneha burst out laughing.

"Sweetheart…this child looks like he fought lunch."

Rohan looked offended.

"I TRIED!"

Sneha kissed his forehead.

"I know."

The Generational Glitch

One Sunday, Rohan's father visited.

The baby started fussing, and Rohan instinctively picked him up, patted his back, and soothed him in seconds.

His father stared like Rohan had grown a second head.

"You're doing all this?
When did men start doing baby work?"

Sneha froze.

Rohan gently rocked the baby and said simply:

"Now".

One word.
Soft, steady, unshakeable.

His father didn't understand it.

But Sneha did.

A generational line had quietly cracked.

The Moment She Saw His Heart

One night, the baby's teething meltdown hit peak misery.

Sneha was exhausted.
Physically.
Emotionally.
Spiritually.

Rohan saw her struggling and gently took the baby.

"Come on champ…Mumma needs a break."

He paced the hall, humming off-key lullabies, rocking the baby like a confused penguin – awkward but determined.

Sneha leaned on the doorway watching him.

Not perfect.
Not magical.
Not Insta-dad material.

But present.

Learning. Trying.

And that mattered more than anything.

The Real Revolution

Later that night, Sneha overheard him whisper to the baby:

"Mumma and Papa share everything.
We're a team, okay?"

A simple line.
No theatrics.
Not cinematic.

But quietly revolutionary.

Rohan hadn't changed overnight.

He hadn't become the feminist hero of the year.
He still messed up, got defensive, forgot things, and sighed loudly while doing dishes.

But he was unlearning.
Relearning.
Showing up.
A soft revolution.

Slow.
Clumsy.
Real.

And that was more than enough.

CHAPTER 18 –
THE REBIRTH OF SNEHA

(Or, How She Slowly Became Herself Again – But Better)

If someone had told Sneha six months ago that she would one day drink chai while it was still hot, she would've laughed, cried, and then accused them of spreading false information.

But here she was.

Chai.
Hot.
No reheating.
No phantom baby cries playing in surround sound.
No guilt.

And that single sip tasted like…victory.

Not the Instagram kind.
The real kind.
The "I survived" kind.

Sneha sat in the balcony; felt something she hadn't felt in months:

Herself.

The Fog Begins To Lift

One afternoon, while scrolling through her phone, Sneha found a picture of herself taken recently – hair messy, top questionable, baby on her hip – and surprisingly, she didn't cringe.

She stared at the photo.

"I look like…me."

Not the pre-baby Sneha.
Not lost Sneha.

A new Sneha.
A stronger Sneha.
A Sneha with more softness and more spine at the same time.

And she liked her.

The Personal Rebellions Begin

Sneha didn't go back to her old habits.
She created new ones – small, delicious rebellions:

- drinking chai without guilt
- taking a 20-minute walk alone
- listening to 90s music loudly
- reading two pages of a book before passing out
- buying herself a proper bra (postpartum friendly, emotionally supportive)
- cooking food SHE liked
- wearing kajal again after months
- sitting alone and breathing
- not explaining every decision
- saying "NO" without melting into guilt
- not over-explaining decisions like she owed the world a PPT.

Small acts.
But together, they felt like quiet revolutions.

The Moment Her Brain Came Back Online

One afternoon, Sneha cracked a joke.

A good one.
A smart one.
A classic Sneha-level sarcastic one.

Rohan laughed so loudly the baby jumped.

Sneha blinked.
"Oh My God…I'm funny again."

It was shocking.

Almost emotional.
Like discovering a long – lost superpower.

She whispered:

"Welcome back, brain".

Her brain whispered back:
"Thank you, madam. Fog was toxic like Delhi winter".

The New Confidence – Not Prettier, But Stronger

Her confidence didn't return with makeup or jeans that finally fit (they still didn't, and she didn't care).

Confidence returned when Sneha stopped.

- apologising for her needs
- over-explaining her choices
- trying to please everyone
- living by "good girl" expectations

- suppressing her emotions
- putting herself last

Sneha became unapologetic –
not loud, not rebellious –
just calm, firm, self-respecting.

A woman who knew her worth because she had rebuilt it brick by brick.

Her Relationship With Her Body Softens

One day she tried on her old jeans.

They refused.

Not politely.
Aggressively.

She laughed – loudly, fully, really.
Not the crying-laugh kind.
Her body wasn't a problem.
It was a story.

A map of survival. A map of motherhood.
A strong, stretched, evolving home.

She touched her stomach and said,
"Thank You for surviving everything."

Acceptance.
A rare, quiet gift.

Sparks of Her Old Passions Return

Sneha wasn't ready to write a book, run a marathon, or invent a startup.

But sparks came back:

Doodling again.
Journalling.
Browsing courses.
Making list of ideas in her notes app.
Feeling tiny flutters of excitement.

She didn't push herself.
She didn't pressure herself.

She simply allowed her inner world to come alive again.

The Conversations Change – Finally Adult Talk

One night after the baby slept, Sneha and Rohan sat together.

Not to discuss diapers.
Not paediatrician.
Not routines.

They talked about:

- old trips
- funny office stories
- dreams for the future
- a movie they wanted to watch
- what their son might grow up to be

It felt…normal.
Warm.

Adult.
Human.

Their friendship, silently sleeping for months, finally woke up.

The First Birthday Looms – And So Does Pride

As the baby approached one year, Sneha found herself reflecting.

What a year.
What a storm.
What a transformation.
She thought of:

- the tears
- the guilt
- the rage
- the breakdown
- the loneliness
- the tiny wins
- the slow healing
- the growth – hers and Rohan's.

She wasn't the woman she used to be.

She was better.
Wiser.
Kinder.
Stronger.
More herself than ever.

Motherhood didn't erase her identity.
It expanded it.

The Rebirth

One night, Sneha stood before the mirror.

Hair messy.
Eyes tired.
Postpartum body real.
Heart full.

She smiled – a soft, victorious smile – and whispered:

"I lost myself this year…
but I found someone stronger."

And for the first time since becoming a mother, she felt whole.

CHAPTER 19 —
THE WISDOM ERA

(Or, How Sneha Went From 'I'm Losing My Mind' to 'I've Got This Mostly…')

Sneha didn't become a Zen monk.
She didn't start doing sunrise yoga.
She didn't read 47 parenting books.

Nothing sensational happened.

But one normal Tuesday morning, something shifted.

The baby spilled an entire bowl of dal on floor – a perfectly executed splash, like modern art in turmeric yellow colour.

Old Sneha would've cried.
Month-4 Sneha would've panicked.
Month-7 Sneha would've yelled, then cried again.

But Month-11 Sneha?

She blinked.
Exhaled.
Picked up the cloth.
Cleaned the mess.
And said calmly:

"Okay. Happens."

Rohan peered from the bedroom like a suspicious meerkat.
"You…okay?"

Sneha smiled.
"Yep."

Terrified, he backed away slowly.
This level of calm in a mother usually means **enlightenment… or the beginning if revolution.**

But Sneha wasn't plotting.
Sneha was just simply…**steady.**

Her brain had returned.
Her heart had softened.
Her identity had rebuilt itself quietly in the background.

She was entering her **Wisdom Era.**

The "I Don't Care At That Level Anymore" Upgrade

A few weeks ago, everything shook her:

comments
mess
opinions
routines
judgements
comparisons
guilt
expectation

Now?
MIL: "Baby is not eating enough."
Sneha: "Okay." (continues eating her poha)

Neighbour: "Your child doesn't wear socks?"
Sneha: "It's 33 degrees outside."

Aunty in lift: "Mine was walking at nine months."
Sneha: "Mine is crawling at his own speed. Good for both of us."

Rohan: "Where are my socks?"
Sneha: "With your brain. Go look for both."

Her emotional reactions had moved from **"daily soap heroine"** to **functional adult human.**

She had finally learnt the secret to modern motherhood:

"Half the things I'm stressed about were not even real problems."

The Calm That Comes From Surviving Agni-Pariksha

Sneha didn't become calm because life got easier.

She became calm because she had survived:

- crying marathons
- teething nightmares
- 3 a.m. existential crisis
- unsolicited advice
- the postpartum guilt Olympics
- her own fears
- Rohan's early aloofness
- Rohan's early attempts at parenting

After that?
A little dal on floor was nothing.

Her meltdown threshold had risen like petrol prices.

Her Humour Returns – Stronger And Sharper

Once when her mother commented,
"Beta, don't pick him up too much. He'll get its habit."

Sneha replied sweetly:
"Even I have habits, nobody is picking me up."

Her mother choked on tea.
Rohan laughed so hard he coughed.
Even the baby clapped like a supportive audience member.

Sneha didn't snap anymore.
She jokingly roasted people instead.
She found humour in nonsense.
Sarcasm became her new superpower.

If anyone judged her, she mentally whispered.

"Unfollow…in real life."

The New Boundaries (Unapologetically)

Sneha began setting boundaries like a queen wearing soft cotton nightwear:

"No visitors today."
"Don't comment on his weight."
"We're doing a different routine."
"I won't force feed him."
"Please ask before picking him up."
"I'm resting. Handle him for ten minutes."

Once upon a time, she would've worried:

"What will they say?"

Now her energy was:

"If they don't like it, they know where the door is."

Other Moms Start Reaching Out

In the building WhatsApp group, suddenly Sneha became the wise one.

She didn't post motivational quotes.
She didn't pretend motherhood was easy.
She was honest.

And honesty attracts tired women like fresh samosas attract office employees.

A new mom messaged her:
"Is it normal to want to cry randomly?"

Sneha replied:
"100%. Welcome to motherhood private limited. You're doing great."

Another mom asked:
"How did you survive teething?"

Sneha:
"I didn't. I died and resurrected."

Sneha, who once felt lost, was now the one giving anchors.
Full Circle.

Her Relationship with Rohan Matures Too

Not perfect.
Not filmy.
Just better.

They snapped less.
Laughed more.
Said sorry faster.
Worked as a team.
Shared small responsibilities.
Held each other without tracking points.

One night, Rohan said:

"You're stronger now."

Sneha replied:

"I had to be."

And it wasn't sad.
It was real.
And empowering.

The Baby's Love Blanket

One afternoon, while Sneha sat on the floor folding tiny clothes, her baby crawled up to her and rested his head on her lap.

No reason.
No need.
Just…love.

Sneha froze.

Her throat tightened.

This – THIS – was motherhood finally touching her heart without chaos in the background.

Not the forced love of postpartum.
Not the fearful love of early months.
Not the exhausted love of teething days.

This was the warm, deep, slow-cooked love that appears only after a year of surviving together.

Sneha stroked his hair and whispered:
"I didn't become a mother the day you were born…I became one slowly – one messy day at a time."

The Golden Truth of Her Wisdom Era

At bedtime, Sneha wrote in her journal:

"I didn't become stronger because I had no choice. I became stronger because I finally chose myself."

She closed the diary with a soft, victorious smile – The smile of a woman who finally, finally feels whole.

The storm had passed.
The fog had lifted.

And Sneha wasn't just surviving motherhood anymore.

She was living it – on her own terms.

CHAPTER 20 –
THE TRUTH BOMB

(Or, The Things nobody Tells You About Motherhood… Until You've Already Lost Your Mind.)

Sneha always thought she was an honest person.

Honest in office.
Honest with friends.
Honest about her pani puri spice levels.

But motherhood?
Motherhood turned her into a professional liar.

Not malicious lies.
Not manipulative lies.

The polite lies.
The socially approved lies.

"Motherhood is beautiful!"
(Translation: I haven't slept in 6 months, save me.)

"I'm loving every minute."
(Lies. All lies.)

"He's such an easy baby!"
(HAA. Aunty, this child has moods like an Indian Monsoon.)

Sneha repeated these lines because that's what new mothers are expected to say – **the script of "good mom energy".**

Until one day, a relative gushed,
"You must be glowing! Babies bring so much joy!"

Sneha nodded politely.

Inside her brain whispered:
"Nonsense."

That was the moment she realised:

She had been censoring her entire motherhood experience.
And she was done.

Done being polite.
Done hiding exhaustion.
Done pretending motherhood was a pastel-coloured ad film.
Done sugarcoating the most brutally honest job in the world.

So, she started saying the truth – softly, sweetly, savagely, depending on the audience.

The Lies Society Sold Her (And the Truths Underneath)

Sneha started mentally listing the motherhood myths she'd been force-fed like prasad.

LIE # 1:

"Motherhood is magical."

TRUTH

Motherhood is magical for approximately 7 minutes a day. The rest is laundry, tears (yours + baby's) and Googling "Is this normal?"

LIE # 2:

"You'll enjoy every moment."

TRUTH

No one enjoys every moment of anything.
Not even Shah Rukh enjoys every movie he made.

LIE # 3:

"Breastfeeding is natural and easy."

TRUTH

Natural does not mean easy.
Giving birth is natural.
Earthquakes are natural.
Both hurt like hell.

For some women, it flows easily.
For others, it's a battlefield—with nipples as collateral damage.

LIE # 4:

"Good Mothers don't get angry."

TRUTH

Good mothers get angry. RAGE.
Sometimes over wet towels.

Sometimes over life.

Good mothers are basically working in rage management + emotional CPR full time.

They're not "losing control."
They're managing emotions at scale.

Anger is data.
It points to a crossed line.

Good mothers don't suppress it.
They respond—and set the boundary.

LIE # 5:

"You'll bounce back."

TRUTH

Some bodies return. Some transform.
Some changes fade with time. Others stay.
None of this is failure.

Body is not a problem to fix, but a story to Honor.
Sneha's body was still negotiating its lease terms.

And Yes, The ONLY thing bouncing in the house is baby.

LIE # 6:

"Your husband will help."

TRUTH

Husbands evolve slower than baby.
But also – they DO evolve (with reminders, Swiggy and Therapy).

LIE #7:

"Once the baby sleeps, you can rest."

TRUTH

One the baby sleeps, you become an unpaid night-shift worker doing dishes, pumping, folding clothes, and questioning her life choices.

LIE # 8:

"Babies thrive on routine".

TRUTH

Baby thrives on chaos. **Routine?** That's just a fancy word moms use to feel in control for 14 minutes a day.

LIE # 9:

"Babies sleep for 8-10 hrs. Sleep when he sleeps."

TRUTH

Babies are Viru Sahastrabuddhe's Fanclub permanent members.
Seven minutes of sleep and they wake up fresh. You, meanwhile, are still deciding whether lying down is worth it.

LIE # 10:

"Postpartum is just a phase."

TRUTH

Postpartum is a personality change, a hormonal earthquake, a spiritual breakdown, and a glow up all happening at once, together!

LIE # 11:

"Postpartum depression happens to "other women."

TRUTH

It can happen to any woman.
Strong, weak, brave, nervous –
PPD doesn't check resumes.
It WALKS in quietly and sits on your chest.

LIE # 12:

"Marriage automatically strengthens after a baby."

TRUTH

A baby doesn't fix anything.
It magnifies every crack, amplifies every silence, and exposes every imbalance.
If the foundation is shaky, motherhood becomes the earthquake.

LIE # 13:

"Motherhood is the best phase of a woman's life."

TRUTH

It is beautiful,
but is also the hardest, messiest, most disorienting identity shift – and not all beauty may feel good.

LIE # 14:

"Women were born for this."

TRUTH
Instinct starts the journey.
Learning sustains it.
No one is born for round-the-clock caregiving,
isolation, sleep deprivation, and identity loss.

Women aren't "built for this."
They rise to it.
Motherhood is Learned.

LIE # 15:

"Breastfeeding proves you are a good mother."

TRUTH

Breastfeeding proves nothing except biology.

Formula milk isn't failure. It's nourishment, backed by science.

Love isn't measured in millilitres.
A bottle never damaged a baby—
But **pressure and guilt have damaged countless mothers.**

LIE # 16:
"If you go back to work, the baby will forget you. You are selfish".

TRUTH

The baby won't forget her. The baby will be fine. But the world will happily forget her if she quits everything.
Women don't choose rent, sanity; and an identity that isn't limited to washing bottles. **It's the world that can't handle a woman who refuses to shrink.**

LIE # 17:

"Every woman eventually wants a baby – it's nature."

TRUTH

No.
Some women want babies.
Some women want peace.
Some women want freedom.
All three are valid – none requires explanation.
Motherhood is a choice, not a compulsory life upgrade.

LIE # 18:

"Mothers don't break."

TRUTH

They do
They shatter silently because the world only checks the baby's temperature, never the mother's pulse. A mother's breakdown is treated like a bad behaviour – not the medical emergency it often is.

LIE #19:

"A supportive husband is a bonus, not a necessity."

TRUTH

No!!!!
A supportive partner is basic infrastructure – like electricity.
Without it; everything crashes, burns, and goes dark.
"Mothers manage alone" is not admiration – its abandonment packaged as strength.

LIE # 20:

"Mothers don't need boundaries."

TRUTH

Everyone respects a working man's boundaries.
A mother's boundaries get treated like optional suggestions.
She's expected to be available 24x7 – to the baby, to the in-laws, to society, to everyone except herself.

LIE # 21:

"Fathers' job is earning; Mother's job is everything."

TRUTH

That's not partnership –
that's a generational scam sold as 'tradition'.
Kids don't need a walking wallet and a burnt-out mother.
They need **two present parents.**
Two adults doing the emotional, mental, physical, and invisible work of raising a human.
Providing money is a contribution –
But parenting is partnership.

Sneha didn't feel guilty saying these truths.
She felt…free.

Honesty, once her trademark, was her new OXYGEN.

No Filters. No Sugarcoating. No Guilt

When someone hinted her baby was "too attached to her," Sneha proudly said:

"That means I'm doing something right."

When a relative commented,
"You look tired,"

Sneha replied:
"I AM tired. I have a baby. What's your excuse?"

Rohan nearly choked on chai.

Sneha didn't feel guilty anymore.
She felt…honest.

And honestly, honesty was fun.

The Deeper Truths She Finally Understood

Between jokes and sarcasm, Sneha uncovered truths that were not funny at all –

Truths she wished someone had warned her about:

- Mothers disappear in the first year. Completely.
- Society celebrates the baby and forgets the mother.
- Mental health silently bleeds inside Indian homes
- Nuclear families exhaust women in ways nobody recognises.
- Women are expected to smile through exhaustion.
- Both working moms and SAHMs are judged equally.
- Marriage cracks before it heals.
- Some postpartum body changes are permanent in some places – and that's okay.
- The guilt never leaves; you just learn to ignore it.
- Motherhood is not instinct. It's skill + patience + survival.

These truths were not meant to scare anyone.
They were meant to **prepare.**

Sneha wished someone had prepared her.

So, she decided she would never let another mother feel blindsided.

The Truths That Are Softer – But Just As Real

Motherhood wasn't just chaos and exhaustion. It was also:

- a tiny head resting on your chest
- a giggle that fixes everything.
- Sleepy cuddles that melt the day's pain
- Love so big it feels terrifying
- Growth one never imagined.

Motherhood wasn't one thing.

It is **everything – mess, magic, exhaustion, joy.**

The Day Sneha Stopped Censoring Herself

A new mom in the building asked her:

"How is motherhood?"

For the first time, Sneha didn't rehearse the polite script.

She said simply, truthfully:

"It's the hardest thing I've ever done.
But it's also the thing that made me meet myself."

The mom stared.
Then exhaled – the relieved exhale of a woman who thought she was failing.
"Thank you", she whispered. "I thought I was the only one struggling."

Sneha smiled.

"That's what they want us to think.
But trust me – you're doing great."

The Truth of Her Life Now

That night, Sneha wrote in her journal:

"Motherhood didn't break me.
It stripped me.
And in that raw painful space...
I finally met myself."

And for the first time, Sneha wasn't scared of the truth.

She was proud of it.

CHAPTER 21 – THE GUILT DETOX

(Or, How Sneha Finally Set Herself Free)

Guilt is sneaky.

It doesn't enter like a thief,
or a villain,
or a sensational soap-operatic "dun-dun-dun" moment.

It tiptoes in quietly.
Sits on your shoulder.
And whispers:

"You could've done better."

Sneha had carried that whisper for a whole year.

Until one random Wednesday afternoon, when the baby threw his snack on the floor for the fourth time, she raised her voice
– a little louder than she meant to.

The baby's eyes widened.
Sneha's heart cracked.

And instantly, guilt pounced.

Not mild guilt.
Not "oops" guilt.

Full Saas Bahu Serial tragedy guilt.
She scooped him up, kissed his face, and whispered,
"I'm Sorry, baby…I'm so sorry."

But then something unexpected happened.

She caught her reflection in the mirror —
Tired, human, doing her best –
and realised:

The guilt wasn't coming from motherhood.
It was coming from the lies she'd been told about motherhood.

And she was done carrying it.

The Guilt List (Longer Than Her Amazon Order History)

Sneha sat down and mentally made a list of everything she had felt guilty about this year.

It was…long.

Absurdly long.

She felt guilty for:

- working too much
- not working enough
- feeding solids
- not feeding enough
- screen-time
- no screen-time
- losing her temper
- being too soft
- wanting a break
- not wanting a break
- sleeping late
- waking up tired
- wanting help

- pretending she didn't want help
- leaving the baby with Rohan
- not trusting the system (Rohan)
- missing milestones
- obsession over milestones
- eating her favourite food
- not eating healthy enough
- giving puree
- giving finger foods
- giving biscuits
- giving up

Basically, **guilt** was the background music of her entire year.

"I cannot believe I tortured myself like this" laugh.
Where Did All This Guilt Come From?

Sneha realised the guilt didn't start from her.

It came from:

Society:
"Sacrifice is motherhood."

Movies:
"Mothers never complain."
(Mothers in movies also wake up with eyeliner.)

Relatives:
"Baby comes first."
(Translation: You come last.)

Instagram:
"Be a CEO + a fit mom + a perfect wife + a glowing goddess."
(With one sleepy child who never cries.)

Patriarchy:
"Mothers must handle everything."

Her upbringing:
"Good girls don't make mistakes."

Sneha had inherited guilt like family jewellery – except the jewellery was heavy, outdated, and caused emotional rashes.

The "I'm Allowed to be A Human Moment."

That evening, after the baby slept, Sneha sat on the bed and whispered:

"I am human."

Not a robot.
Not a saint.
Not a sacrificial goddess.
Not a flawless mother.

Just…human.

Allowed to make mistakes.
Allowed to get angry.
Allowed to rest.
Allowed to break.
Allowed to repair.
Allowed to be imperfect.

She felt something loosen inside her chest –

First release of a lifetime of pressure.

The Symbolic Release

Sneha opened the Notes app on her phone –
the one filled with:

- routines she never followed
- schedules she abandoned
- tips she tried once
- perfect-mom plans that broke her
- unrealistic expectations
- mental checklists that only drained her

She hovered over "Delete All."

Took a breath.

Pressed the delete button.

Deleted the guilt.
Deleted the pressure.
Deleted the older and outdated version of herself who thought she had to earn her worth.

It wasn't a spectacle.
But it felt like she had put down a 50 kg of invisible weight from her shoulders.

Rewriting The Definition of A "Good Mother"

That night, she wrote in her journal.

A good mother is not perfect.
A good mother is PRESENT.

A good mother:

- tries

- loves
- nourishes herself
- forgives herself
- asks for help
- laughs
- cries
- rests
- protects her peace
- sets boundaries
- lets her child see she's human
- chooses joy
- chooses herself

A good mother is not a woman who never breaks.

A good mother is a woman wo rebuilds herself – again and again –
while loving a child who has no idea how hard she's working.

The Forgiveness Moment

Sneha closed her eyes and whispered:

"I forgive you."

To herself.

For every meltdown.
For every tear.
For every guilty thought.
For every "not-enough" moment.
For all the comparisons.
For the nights she cried alone.
For doubting herself.

For losing her patience.
For trying to be the version of a mother society forced on her.
For thinking she needed to be perfect.

“I forgive you”, she said again.

And this time she meant it.

Her shoulders softened.
Her breath deepened.
Her chest eased.

Healing had begun, finally!

The Peaceful Realisation

Sneha looked at her sleeping baby and felt something she hadn’t felt all year:

Not guilt.
Not fear.
Not tightness.

Peace.

Real peace.
Not the “baby is finally asleep” peace.

The peace that comes when a woman finally puts down emotional baggage she never needed to carry.

She didn’t want to be the **perfect** mother anymore.
She wanted to be a **happy** mother.

A **healthy** mother.

A **whole** mother.

Sneha whispered into the quiet room:

"I choose me.
And choosing me is choosing him too".

CHAPTER 22 — THE SILENCE BREAKER

(Or, The Things Mothers Think But Never Say Out Loud)

There are parts of motherhood people print on greeting cards –
soft cheeks, tiny socks, baby smell, first smiles, Instagram reels with piano music.

And then there are parts of motherhood no one prints anywhere –
because they're too raw, too messy, too honest, too human.

Sneha had lived both.

But she had never spoken about the second kind.
Not to her mother.
Not to Rohan.
Not to friends.
Not even to herself.

Until now.

No more filters.
No more polite silence.
No more "I'm fine."
No more pretending this journey was only cute and holy.

And now, she was ready to speak – loudly, clearly, unapologetically.

The Night She Never Told Anyone About

Sneha remembered a night from the early months.

The baby had been crying non-stop—
not normal crying,
but opera-level, soul-shattering shrieks that felt like they were vibrating inside her rib cage.

Sneha was exhausted.
Tired down to her bones.
Her body felt stitched together with tiredness and pain she couldn't even admit aloud.

And in a moment of utter overwhelm, Sneha whispered into the darkness:

"I want to disappear."

Not run away.
Not leave forever.

Just…vanish for a bit.

Five minutes.
Ten.
Just enough to breathe.

She never said this to anyone.

Because what would people say?

A mother wanting a break?
A mother wanting silence?
A mother wanting herself?

Unacceptable.

It took several lonely nights for Sneha to understand:

Dark thoughts don't make you a bad mother.

They make you a tired one.
A human one.

The Secret Thoughts Every Mother Hides

Sneha finally admitted the thoughts that had haunted her silently:

"I miss my old life."
"Sometimes the crying drives me mad."
"I don't know what I'm doing."
"Why does everyone think this is natural?"
"Will I ever feel like myself again?"
"Some days I feel nothing."
"Some days I feel too much."
"Sometimes I want someone to come take care of ME."
"Is something wrong with me?"

These thoughts were taboo.
Forbidden.
Unacceptable.

Yet every mother she knew had whispered at least one of these into a pillow.

Sneha realised:

Motherhood wasn't terrifying.
Motherhood in silence was.

The Loneliness Of Being A Mother In India

Sneha thought about how motherhood is treated in India – worshipped but not understood.

Everyone celebrates mothers.
But no one listens to mothers.

Everyone praises sacrifice.
But no one questions why she must do it alone.

Everyone asks about the baby.
No one asks about the mother.

Sneha had been surrounded by advice,
But starved of emotional support.

This silence – not sleep deprivation – is what breaks mothers.

The Good Mother Myth She Finally Destroys

Sneha listed the expectations that were quietly placed on her:

- ✓ A good mother is always patient
- ✓ A good mother never gets angry
- ✓ A good mother doesn't need breaks
- ✓ A good mother bounce back quickly
- ✓ A good mother manages everything
- ✓ A good mother doesn't complain
- ✓ A good mother doesn't cry
- ✓ A good mother is always smiling
- ✓ A good mother sacrifices without resentment

Sneha laughed – a tired, bitter sweet laugh.

This list wasn't motherhood.
This was sainthood packaged as expectation.

And she was not a goddess.
She was a woman.

A tired, loving, flawed, strong woman.

Postpartum Anxiety – The Ghost No One Acknowledges

Sneha remembered the nights she lay awake even when the baby slept.

The intrusive thoughts:

"What if something happens?"
"What if I'm not doing enough?"
"What if I mess up?"

Not depression.
Not breakdowns.

Just constant anxiety.
Quiet, invisible, dismissed by everyone except her own racing heart – A background hum of fear.

Nobody warned her that postpartum anxiety could be:

- silent
- overlooked
- internal
- common
- TREATABLE

But the day she learned the term "postpartum anxiety,"
She felt a weight lift.

Nothing was wrong with her.
Something was happening to her.

And it had a name.

And treatable.
And common.

The Most Honest Thing She Ever Wrote

One evening, Sneha sat with her journal and wrote:

"There were days I didn't feel connected to my baby. And I thought I was failing. I wanted to take baby away."

She cried after writing it –
not out of shame,
but relief.

Because she finally understood clearly:

Connection doesn't always happen at birth.
Sometimes it grows like a seed – slowly, quietly, beautifully.

And that love is just as real.

The Conversation That Healed Her

For the first time, Sneha told Rohan about that early -night thought –
the one where she wanted to disappear.

He didn't judge her.
He didn't gasp.
He didn't blame.

He just held her hand and said:

"You should've told me.
We would've handled it together."

It wasn't romantic.
It wasn't dramatic.

It was human. Real. Healing.

Rohan added softly:

"You weren't alone, Sneha.
You just felt alone."

She nodded, tears rolling down her cheeks freely, as she felt allowed to be vulnerable without being judged.

She didn't hide them, she let them flow.

Finally.

The Line That Frees Her

Sneha finally understood:

She was not a bad mother.
She was a silenced mother.

There's a difference.

A huge one.

A life-giving one.

The Most Courageous Thing She Says All Year

She faced the mirror – messy hair, tired eyes, soft belly but strong heart –

without fear, without shame:

"Motherhood didn't break me.
Silence did.
I'm not staying silent anymore."

And with that, something heavy, ancient, and inherited finally lifted.

Sneha had broken the last taboo.
She had reclaimed her voice.
And she walked out of that silence a different woman,

A freer one.
A truer one.
A whole one.

CHAPTER 23—
THE REINVENTION
(Or, Why Sneha Didn't "Go Back" – She Went Forward)

The calendar notification blinked on her phone like a tiny digital demon.

"Return to Work – 10 days left."

Earlier in the year, this reminder had felt like a punch in the stomach.
But today?

Sneha stared at it with a strange new feeling.

Not panic.
Not guilt.
Not dread.

Clarity.

For the first time since her baby arrived, Sneha didn't feel pressured by the reminder.
She felt…powerful.

The old Sneha would've immediately asked:
"How do I fit into their expectations?"

But the new Sneha asked:
"What do I want?"

The Three Roads

Sneha sat with her journal and did what postpartum Sneha never had the mental energy to do – think clearly.

She wrote three options:

Option 1: Go back full-time (like nothing happened)

Pros:

- Money
- Identity
- Professional rhythm

Cons:

- Baby care stress
- Burnout risk
- No flexibility
- Emotional overload

Sneha made a face.
Her energy said "no thank you."

Option 2: Quit completely

Pros:

- Peace
- Time with baby

Cons:

- Losing part of herself
- Depending solely on Rohan
- Future uncertainty

Old Sneha would've picked this out of guilt.

New Sneha refused to shrink herself.

Option 3: Reinvent work-life – HER way

Pros:

- Balance
- Identity
- Flexibility
- Autonomy

Cons:

- Requires planning
- New learning
- Slight chaos
- Courage

Sneha circled this option.

Boldly.
Decisively.

She whispered:

**"I'm not going back.
I'm moving forward."**

Rohan's Reaction – Realistic, Not Fairytale

That evening, Sneha told Rohan her thoughts.

He didn't say,
"Follow your dreams, my queen!"
or
"Quit your job, I'll handle everything!"

Please – Rohan was still Rohan.

He looked thoughtful and said:

"Let's think this through.
What do you want your days to look like?"

And yes… EMI's will continue, expenses will increase, and you would be earning less.
But I'm in it with you."

Not flashy encouragement.
Not patriarchal worry.

Practical Partnership.
Planning.
Genuine support.

She appreciated it more than any wedding day vows.

The Inner Clarity She Didn't Know She Had

That night, while brushing her teeth, Sneha had an epiphany:
She didn't want her old job.
She didn't want her old life.

She wanted a new version of both.

A Version with:

- mental space
- fewer hours
- meaningful work
- flexibility
- autonomy

- financial independence
- sanity
- and to NEVER AGAIN lose herself

Motherhood had rewritten her identity.
Work would need to adjust accordingly.

The Boss Call (No Fear, Only Power)

Sneha scheduled a call with her boss.

Her heart did the mild dhak-dhak.
but her voice was steady.

"Hi, I'm ready to return…
but not the way I left.
I'd like to discuss a flexible model that works for both of us."

Silence.

Sneha panicked internally for 0.5 seconds.

Then her boss said:

"I'm glad you said this.
Let's explore options."

They discussed:

- phased return
- hybrid working
- project based responsibilities
- predictable hours
- boundaries around late calls
- a realistic workload

Sneha ended the call feeling something she hadn't felt in months:

Respected
Seen
Equal

She wasn't negotiating like a desperate employee.
She was negotiating like a woman who had rebuilt her worth.

She Creates a New Life Like: A CEO of Her Life

Sneha drafted her new rules:

No over-functioning.
No martyrdom.
No guilt.
No "I'll do it all."

She drafted a structure:

- Office work during defined hours
- Dedicated family time
- Daily break for herself
- Shared responsibilities with Rohan
- Clear division of chores
- Childcare plan that didn't break her spirit

She wrote at the top:

"I refuse to burn out again."

Motherhood had taught her exactly where her limits were.
She wasn't crossing them.

A Practical But Beautiful Conversation With Herself

Sneha looked at the mirror – not searching for flaws, but checking alignment.

She asked, "What kind of life do you want?"

The answer was simple and clean:

"A life that supports me.
Not a life I need to recover from."

Her decision was solid and her chest felt light.

The First Morning of Her New Life

The next morning, Sneha opened her laptop.
Her baby played beside her, banging a spoon against a bowl like a musical genius.

She didn't feel overwhelmed.
She felt centred.

She didn't feel like she was abandoning him.
She felt like she was reclaiming herself.

She didn't feel fear.
She felt purpose.

Sneha realised:

She wasn't returning to her old world.
She was creating a new one –
curated, balanced, self-chosen.

A life built by:

- love
- clarity
- boundaries
- partnership
- And practical systems that protected her peace.

Sneha smiled – a confident, peaceful smile – and whispered:

"You're doing this, girl."

And she was.

Because now, she finally had a support structure that didn't drown her:

On days she had meeting outside, her house- help stepped in without fuss.
On tougher days, Rohan promised to rearrange his schedule – not perfectly, but sincerely – as long as she told him in advance.
Technology filled the remaining gaps: the baby-camera app on her phone, the breast pump packed neatly in her tote, the milk storage bags labelled like a tiny dairy empire.

This wasn't chaos anymore.

This was a system – one built intentionally, gently, confidently.

The rebirth of her career had begun – **not on society's schedule, but on hers.**

CHAPTER 24 – MARRIAGE 2.0

(Or, How Sneha and Rohan Finally became the Teammates, Not Co-survivors.)

The house was unusually peaceful.

The baby was stacking cups in the corner –
not crying, not screaming, not demanding a human -shaped carrier.
Just…stacking.

Rohan stood nearby, folding tiny shirts in the most geometrically incorrect way imaginable, while Sneha sat on the rug, working on her laptop, sipping hot chai (yes, hot again – the universe was finally respecting her).

For the first time in months the home didn't feel like a battleground.
It felt like…life.

Sneha looked around and thought:

"This finally feels like a home again."

Not perfect.
Not spotless.
Not Instagrammable.

But warm.
Soft.
Steady.

Like the fog had lifted.

The Conversation They Didn't Even Know They Needed

Later that night, after putting the baby to sleep (with only two rewinds of "Twinkle Twinkle"), they sat on the balcony.

Not as project managers.
Not as exhausted zombies.

As Sneha and Rohan.
Two adults who once liked each other.
Two adults who forgot that for a while.

Rohan said quietly,
"This year…it was hard on us, na?"

Sneha nodded.
"Yeah. Really hard."

He took a deep breath.
"But we didn't give up."

Sneha smiled.
"We almost did."

He laughed.
"True. But we didn't."

And that small laugh felt like a tiny crack letting sunlight in.

Small Actions, Big Shifts

Rohan wasn't giving monologues about women empowerment.
He didn't transform into a domestic Krishna on a lotus flower.

He just…showed up.

- He made chai for both of them– sometimes voluntarily, sometimes on assignment with mild resistance.
- He packed the diaper bag after confirming the checklist with Sneha twice.
- He wiped the floor after a food spill but after being reminded, but still doing it.
- And he helped with bath time – awkward but present.
- He put away his socks without being told. (This alone deserved national awards.)

Sneha noticed.

Not because these were extraordinary acts – but because this was the first time, she felt like she wasn't single-handedly carrying the entire house on her back.

They still had disagreements.
They still snapped sometimes.
They still misunderstood each other occasionally.

But the recovery was quicker.
Apologies were faster.
Tenderness resurfaced.

This was marriage in real life unfiltered, messy, evolving.

Real Romance, Not Instagram Romance

One evening, while picking up toys, their hands brushed.

They froze.
Embarrassed.

Shy.
Like teenagers caught making eye contact.

Sneha blushed.
Rohan smirked.

"You look…calmer these days," he said.

Sneha laughed. "I am. And it's not because life got easier. I just stopped drowning."

He nodded.
"I can see that. I feel it too."

There was silence –
the comfortable kind you earn back with effort.

They sat close on the sofa that night.
Not holding hands.
Not cuddling.
Just sitting close.

Sometimes intimacy returns not with kisses…but with comfort.

The Micro-Fight That Proved They Had Grown.

Two days later, Rohan forgot to bring home the detergent.

Old Sneha: meltdown.
Old Rohan: defensive ego monologue.

New them:

Sneha: "You forgot?"
Rohan: "Yeah. I'll go now."

Sneha: "It's late. Tomorrow is fine."
Rohan: "Okay."

That was it.

No drama.
No emotional Olympics.
Just basic human communication.

Progress.

The Moment, They Saw Each Other Clearly

One night, after the baby finally knocked out, they sat on the bed scrolling memes.

Rohan showed her one:
"Marriage is two people taking turns being tired."

Sneha laughed.
"True. But now we take turns properly."

He looked at her- really looked.

"You know," he said softly, "I didn't realise how much you were handling. I just…didn't know."

Sneha didn't roll her eyes.
She didn't throw sarcasm.

She simply said,
"I know. And you're trying now."

He nodded.
Relieved.
Seen.

They weren't perfect.
But they were honest.

The Parenting Realisation That Hit Like A Bucket Of Cold Water

A few days later, watching their almost one-year -old chase a ball like a puppy on caffeine overdose, Sneha had a flash of clarity.

She turned to Rohan and whispered:

"You realise…the first year wasn't the job?"
Rohan looked confused.

Sneha explained:
"This was just the **probation period."**

Rohan froze.
Then laughed.
Then froze again.

"Oh my God…You're right."

Sneha continued, wise and declarative:

"Parenting isn't a project. It's a career.
The job description keeps changing
The boss keeps growing.
He keeps demanding with even stricter timelines.
And the work overload? Never ends."

Rohan looked at their energetic child.
"So basically…the real work starts now?"

"Absolutely," Sneha said.

They both burst out laughing—
that exhausted, "we're in this together" laugh.

They weren't scared.

They felt ready.

They had survived colic, teething, postpartum storms, sleep regression, guilt, fights, silence…
and somehow rebuilt themselves in the process.

If they could survive Year 1,
they could survive anything.

Even toddlerhood—
God help them.

Marriage 2.0: Upgraded, Not Perfect.

That night, as they slept with the baby sprawled horizontally between them like a traffic barricade, Sneha looked at Rohan in the dim light.

Not the man she married.
Not the clueless new father.
But the teammate she had earned through fire.

"We'll be okay," she whispered.

Rohan half-asleep murmured,
"We already are."

And Sneha believed him.

Not because everything was fixed.
But because everything was honest.

They weren't going back to their old marriage.

They were building a new one—
stronger, softer, wiser, human.

Marriage 2.0.

CHAPTER 25—
THE NEW MOTHERHOOD MANIFESTO

(Or, Sneha's Rules for Surviving and Thriving in This Lifelong Job)

On the night before her baby's first birthday, Sneha sat on the living-room floor, surrounded by balloons, half-baked decorations, and a very confused one-year-old who was chewing tape like it was gourmet papad.

The house looked like a party store had exploded.
The baby looked delighted.
Sneha looked tired but glowing,
--not Instagram filter glowing
But **earned glowing.**

Her son wobble toward her on unsteady feet, arms wide open, smile bigger than the moon.

He crashed into her lap.

Sneha held him close and felt the truth settle softly in her chest:

One year ago, she became a mother.
Tonight, she finally feels like one.

Not because she mastered routines.
Not because she had "figured it out".
And definitely not because the year was easy or magical.

But because she:
survived it.
Grew through it.
Evolved with it.

And for the first time since giving birth.
she didn't feel like she was losing herself.

She felt like she was becoming herself.

#1. Parenting Is Not a Project – It's a Lifelong Career

Sneha kissed the top of her baby's head.

"What a year," she whispered.
"The longest probation period of my life."

Everyone said the same thing:
"First year is hardest."
"Once they turn one, it gets easy."
"Bas, toddlerhood is fun!"

Fun?
Had they seen toddlers?

Sneha had gotten a preview of toddler chaos – the speed, the climbing, the opinions, the toddler logic, the meltdowns.

Fun?
Sure.
If you were an Olympic athlete with the patience of a Buddhist monk.

She realised something powerful:

Year One wasn't the end.

It was the **orientation + probation + unpaid internship,** all rolled into one.
The real job — the evolving, unpredictable, ever-changing, shape-shifting career of parenting – was only just beginning.

But now?
Sneha wasn't scared.

She was confident and ready –
not because toddlerhood would be easy –
but because **she finally trusted herself.**

#2. Sneha's New Rulebook (The One She Wishes She Had)

She opened her journal – the same one that had survived tears, therapy, guilt, laughter, and tiny banana stains – and wrote her own rules.

Not society's.
Not an aunty's.
Not Instagram's

HERS.

She titled it:

"You're Hired, Mommy – The Real Contract."
And she wrote:

- ✓ **Rule#1: A mother is allowed to be human.**
  With flaws, fears and needs.

- ✓ **Rule#2: Asking for help is not failure.**
  It is intelligent delegation.

- ✓ **Rule#3: You don't lose yourself after motherhood.**
  You expand, stretch and evolve.

- ✓ **Rule#4: Your body is not a 'bounce back' project.**
  It is a lived-in, life-built home.

It deserves gratitude, not judgement.

- ✓ **Rule#5: Perfection is a scam.**
  Being "Present" is enough.
  Being "Loving" is enough.
  Bring "Alive and trying" is enough.

- ✓ **Rule#6: Motherhood is a skill learned daily**
  You will make mistakes.
  You will adjust and learn.
  And your job description will change every month.

- ✓ **Rule#7: Guilt is noise put into women's heads.**
  You get to Turn the volume down.

- ✓ **Rule#8: Marriage will shift, crack, stretch…then strengthen**
  Let it evolve.

- ✓ **Rule#9: You matter outside your child.**
  Your dreams.
  Your rest.
  Your time.
  Your joy.

- ✓ **Rule#10: You are doing enough.**
  More than enough.
  Always have been.

Sneha looked at the list and felt tears roll down her cheeks –

not sad tears.
Not tired tears.

Tears of recognition.

This was her truth now.

#3. A Soft Moment That Closed the Year.

The baby crawled into her lap again, babbling in baby-language, clapping like he had just discovered the concept of applause.

Sneha kissed his head.

"I didn't become a mother the day you were born", she whispered.
"I became one little by little…one messy, exhausting, beautiful day at a time."

He looked up at her like she was his whole universe.
And in his eyes, Sneha saw the whole year:

The fear.
The rage.
The love.
The breakdown.
The healing.
The becoming.

#4. What Sneha Would Tell Every New Mom

She imagined a mother out there – tired, confused, scared, overwhelmed – the way she once was.

And she wished she could sit beside her and say:

"You don't have to be perfect.
You don't have to be strong every day.
You don't have to love every moment.

You don't have to lose yourself to be a good mother. You just have to show up – Honestly, Imperfectly, Humanly."

"You're doing better than you think."

#5. Sneha's Promise – To Herself, and to Him

She held her son close and whispered"

"I will raise you with love—
But I will raise myself with love too."

"I will protect your happiness –
But I will protect mine too."

"I will be your mother –
But I will also be me."

This was Sneha's rebirth.
Her second beginning.

FULL CIRCLE

At midnight, Sneha blew out the single candle on her son's tiny cake.

Rohan hugged both of them.
The baby squealed.
The year turned.

Sneha smiled – a deep peaceful smile that came from her bones.

She whispered into the dim-warm room:

**"Motherhood didn't complete me.
It expanded me."**

And just like that,
The probation period ended.

She was no longer a scared new hire.

She was a mother. – strong, wise, soft, evolving.

Ready for whatever came next.

EPILOGUE
The Parenting Performance Review (Self-Appraisal)

Employee: Sneha (Mother)
Position: Primary Caregiver, Chaos Manager, Emotional Shock Absorber
Department: Motherhood Division
Reporting Manager: Baby (The CEO)

Key Achievements:

- ✓ Kept tiny human alive and rocking (100% success rate)
- ✓ Learned 47 new skills without any training
- ✓ Decoded 17 different types of cries
- ✓ Didn't quit even when every cell screamed to
- ✓ **Major Milestone:** Asked for Help
- ✓ **Revolutionary Act:** Set boundaries
- ✓ **Unheard of Act:** Chose self sometimes
- ✓ Kept marriage alive despite near death experiences
- ✓ Built village from scratch
- ✓ Stayed mostly 'sane', definition of 'sane' adjusted accordingly

AREAS FOR IMPROVEMENT

- Still comparing self to Instagram mothers
- Occasional rage episodes (frequency decreasing)
- Guilt Management needs work
- Self-Care compliance – 40% (up from 0%)
- House Organisation: erratic (but functional)

COMPETENCIES DEMONSTRATED

- Crisis Management: Expert Level
- Multitasking: Olympic Gold Standard
- Functioning on No Sleep: PhD Level
- Self-Advocacy: Beginner (But trying)
- Partnership Building (In progress)

Overall Rating: ★★★★★ **(5/5)**

Exceeds Expectations: *Employee has demonstrated exceptional resilience, adaptability and survival skills under extreme conditions. Has proven she's human – which is exactly right.*

Contract Renewal

- Automatic and Permanent.
- No Exit clause, you're hired for Life.
- **Promotion: Approved**
- **Perks & Benefits:** Toothless Smiles, tiny hand Squeezes, Unconditional Love and yes, Personal Discovery and Growth

FINAL NOTE FROM SNEHA

Would I hire myself again?

Ask me in eighteen years.

But for now: **Yes, absolutely Yes**
Not because I'm perfect.

Because,

I'm REAL.

And REAL is the only qualification this job actually needs.

BONUS CHAPTER 1— THE MOMENTS THAT MADE IT WORTH IT

(Or, The Tiny Joys That Saved Sneha When Nothing Else Could)

Motherhood wasn't just made of sleepless nights, hormonal tsunamis, or Google searches that should've been illegal.

It was also built on tiny, ridiculous, heart-expanding moments –
the ones that arrived without announcement,
the ones that didn't trend online,
the ones that somehow held Sneha together when she was falling apart.

Tonight, on the eve of her baby turning one, she finally allowed herself to relive those moments—the ones that made every meltdown, every tear, every sleepless night…worth It.

---

1. **The Very First Touch (Birth – Week 1)**
   Kangaroo care – the moment that rewired her entire heart.

The first time they placed him on her bare chest, Sneha felt something she didn't have words for.

He wasn't smiling.
He wasn't cute.
He wasn't peaceful.
He was angry-red, squishy, furious at being born.

But when his cheek touched her skin…
he melted.

His fists unclenched.
His breathing synced with hers.

And Sneha – stitched, shaking, overwhelmed – felt a calm she hadn't felt in months.

It was like her heart whispered:
"Here he is. Here you are."

That moment alone carried her through many dark nights ahead.

---

2. The Milk-Drunk Smile (Week 3)

Half asleep, half hungry, fully melodramatic –this child learned early how to charm.

One night at 3:17 a.m., in the middle of the feeding, he suddenly paused…
looked up at her…
and gave a crooked, lazy, half sleep smile.

Milk bubbled at the corner of his mouth.
His eyes crossed because he was drowsy.
He looked drunk on life.

Sneha forgot the tears in her eyes, the ache in her back, the cracking in her brain.
THAT one tiny smile?
Enough dopamine to keep her alive for three days.

---

3. The Startled Limbs Dance (Week 5)

There is something spectacular about how babies get scared of their…own limbs.

Sneha would put him down gently – VERY gently – and he'd react like:

"WHO THREW MY ARMS?!"

Hands shooting out.
Legs kicking.
Eyes wide.
Drama queen behaviour.

Sneha laughed every single time.

It was the first comedy routine of many.

---

4. The First Giggle (Month 2)

Not a cute smile.
Not a tiny chuckle.

A *full, shocked, belly giggle* –
because Sneha sneezed too loudly.

That was it.
That was the joke.
He froze.
Sneha froze.
Then he erupted into laughter like she was the funniest person alive.

She spent the next three days trying to recreate the sneeze.
He refused.

Babies:1
Parents: 0

---

5. The Fountain Spit-Up Talent (Month 3)

One morning, when Rohan lifted him high like Simba, the baby released a perfect arc of spit-up.

A FOUNTAIN.
Like India Gate Water Show.
Directly into Rohan's beard.

Sneha had to lie down on the floor because she was laughing so hard.

That was the day their child was nicknamed:
"The Milk Volcano".

---

6. The Mimicking Phase Begins (Month 4)

Sneha yawned.
He yawned.

Sneha stuck her tongue out.
He stuck HIS tongue out.

Sneha tried to say "Ooo."
He replied "Ooo" like a baby owl attending rehearsal.

Instant serotonin.
Instant friendship.
Immediate heart explosion.

---

7. The Attempted Rolling (Month 5)

He tried to roll over with the confidence of a gymnast…and *With the stability of a potato.*

He'd swing his legs energetically,
lift one shoulder with determination….
then flop back like a defeated samosa.

Sneha cheered anyway.
He looked pleased with his own nonsense.

---

8. The First Solids – AKA The Food Slapstick Era (Month 6)

Carrot puree?
Rejected.

Banana?
On the floor.
Dal water?
On Sneha's kurta.

But the highlight?

Sneha said "Aaaaa."
He said "Aaaaa" back…
then BLEW a raspberry, launching food like a fountain straight into her face.

They stared at each other.
He burst out laughing.

Sneha did too.

This moment healed something in her –
a reminder that joy could be messy too.

---

9. The Kangaroo Nap That Changed Everything (Month 7)

He had a gassy day.
Sneha had a weepy day.

She tucked him against her chest – skin against skin – and swayed gently.

He sighed.
Slept instantly.
Arms wrapped around her like a tiny koala.

Sneha felt her heartbeat slow.
Her mind quiet.
Her soul settle.

Kangaroo care didn't just soothe him.
It healed her.

---

10. The Scooting Adventures (Month 8)

He wasn't crawling yet.
He was…scooting.

Meaning:
He dragged himself backward like a confused crab.

Sneha placed toys in front of him.
He scooted away from them.
Frustrated.
Offended.
Dramatic.

Sneha laughed until her stomach hurt.

---

11. The Peek-a-boo Obsessed Phase (Month 9)

He discovered curtains.

He'd hide.
Sneha would say, "Where did baby go?"
And he'd burst out like:

"Surprise, I'm Here, Do Not Panic."

This happened 47 times daily.
Sneha loved all 47.

---

12. The "I Found My Voice" Phase (Month 10)

He started babbling nonstop –
Louder than pressure cooker whistles.

"Pa pa pa!"
"Mama ma maaa!"
"Ta ta ta taaaaaaaaa!"

And the famous baby-screech—
a sound capable of cracking marble.

But one day, after a long babble monologue,
he pressed his forehead to Sneha's and whispered soft sleepy sounds.

The kind of baby talk that melts adult bones.

---

13. The Toddler Comedy Level Unlock (Month 11)

He began copying EVERYTHING:

Sneha sneezed → he responded with a fake "achoo" that had more drama than a daily soap.

She cleared her throat → he cleared his like a 75-year-old uncle watching TV.

Rohan laughed loudly → he laughed louder, mocking him.

Both of them had never loved being mocked more.

---

14. The Ultimate Joy – His First Steps Towards Her (Month 12)

He held the sofa.
Looked at her.
Wobbled.
Wobbled more.

Then took one brave, tiny, miraculous step.

Not towards a toy.
Not towards Rohan.

Towards *her*.

Arms wide.
Eyes shining.
Trust overflowing.

He reached her and collapsed into her lap like a soft, triumphant potato.

Sneha kissed him all over and whispered:
"Every hard day…was worth this moment."

And she meant it.

---

15. The Full Circle Moment Before One

As she tucked him in that night,
his tiny hand reached for her finger –
the same way he had done on day one.

Instant flashback.
Instant softness.
Instant meaning.

Sneha felt the entire year blur into one truth:

Motherhood didn't become worth it all at once. It became worth it moment by moment.

The ridiculous ones.
The healing ones.
The funny ones.
The heart-stopping ones.

All woven into a year she would never forget.

BONUS CHAPTER 2—
THINGS MY INFANT THINKS ARE LEGAL

(Or, Why My Child Believes He Is Exempt from All Indian Laws and Common Sense)

By the end of Sneha's first year as a mother, she realised something important:

Her baby did not think he was a baby.
Her baby thought he was a ***free citizen of the universe with zero rules, zero boundaries, and full diplomatic immunity.***

Here is a non-exhaustive list of things her infant believes are not only allowed…
but **strongly encouraged** by the Indian Government.

---

1. **Biting the hand that feeds you— literally.**
   Breast, bottle, finger, shoulder…
   Any human flesh is fair game.

2. **Waking up violently cheerful at 5:01a.m.**
   As if he had a job at the stock market.
   As if his mother slept at 9 p.m. and not 3:40 a.m.

3. **Pulling out clumps of hair like it's a team sport**
   Mother's scalp = public property

4. **Slapping the parent who is comforting you**
   Cry
   Get lifted.
   Deliver slap.

Repeat.

5. **Screaming bloody murder because the banana broke.**
   The banana broke → democracy collapsed → world ended → how dare mother live.

6. **Pressing random buttons including:**
   - TV power
   - AC temperature
   - Lift alarm
   - Mother's mental alarm

   Every button is meant for pressing,
   Especially the expensive ones.

7. **Eating dust but rejecting gourmet food**
   Organic puree? NO
   Dal-Chawal? NO
   Apple-Carrot-Dates Pudding? NO
   Floor-tile flavour? **YES CHEF.**

8. **Climbing furniture like he has a rock-climbing subscription**
   Sofa→ table → window grill.
   Every surface is Everest to be scaled.

9. **Throwing food even if he likes it.**
   The law is simple:
   If I can throw it, I must throw it.

   Bonus points for hitting parent's face.

10. **Making eye contact while doing something illegal.**
    Then smiling.
    Then continuing.

11. **Conducting midnight scream concerts.**

    At 2 a.m.
    At 3 a.m.
    At 4 a.m.

    Because why should neighbours sleep when he isn't.

12. **Grabbing spectacles like he's auditioning for WWE.**
    Rohan's glasses did not survive.
    Sneha's dignity did not survive.

13. **Suddenly going limp when being picked up.**
    The famous Baby Noodles Move.
    Illegal. Unnecessary. Frequent.

14. **Switching from angel to demon in 0.4 seconds.**
    One moment: smiling cherub.
    Next moment: screaming banshee.
    No explanation. No apology.

15. **Crawling faster when you say "NO".**
    "No" = "Catch me if you can!"

16. **Treating remote controls, slippers, and wires as gourmet snacks.**

Mango? No.
Mobile Charging Cable? DELICIOUS.

17. **Try to dive off the bed every 14 minutes.**
    As if gravity is a suggestion.

18. **Touching the dog's tail, cat's food, and every single dustbin.**
    Nature's call to babies:
    "If it's unhygienic, touch it."

19. **Slapping their own reflection.**
    Who is this baby?
    Why is he copying me?
    Must Attach.

20. **Laughing after committing a crime**
    Pull hair→ laugh
    Throw toy at face →laugh
    Poop at the exact moment diaper is removed→ laugh louder

    And the greatest crime of all…

21. **Stealing your heart every single day**
    Repeatedly.
    Shamelessly.
    Without remorse.
    Without intention of returning it.

SECTION II: In Her Own Words

In Her Own Words"

Stories from mothers who chose to speak. Read them slowly. They may feel familiar.

Before I asked other mothers to speak, I had to speak myself.
Not as an expert. Not as someone who had figured it out.
But as a woman who had survived motherhood twice — in two very different ways.
This is why I listened. This is why this chapter exists.

I Survived Motherhood Twice — In Two Very Different Ways

— Pallavi Raj, Chennai (Author's own story)

I have two daughters.
And two very different beginnings as a mother.

The first came in 2019.
Life around me looked fine. People were there. Smiles, routines, help.
But inside, I was unravelling quietly.

I was tired in a way sleep didn't fix.
I cried without knowing why.
I felt lonely even when the room was full.

I kept telling myself it was nothing.
A haircut would help.
Changing the house would help.
If I just looked better, felt busier, it would pass.

It didn't.

For months, I lived in denial — because where I come from, only "mental" people see psychiatrists. And I wasn't that. Or so I told myself.

One afternoon, after an argument I couldn't name and a heaviness I couldn't carry anymore, I took my baby, asked my help to come with me, and stood outside a doctor's chamber. I remember standing there — unsure, ashamed, scared.
When he listened to me, calmly, without rushing or fixing, something inside me broke open.
Just being heard felt like support.

A mild medicine. A counsellor.
Healing didn't come suddenly.
But slowly, I started breathing again.

I told my husband six months later — not because he would have stopped me, but because even then, I wasn't ready to admit how lost I had been.

Life found its rhythm again.

And then, in 2024, I became pregnant once more.
This time, I thought I was prepared.
I wasn't.

One-night, past midnight, something felt wrong.
Water leaking. Panic rising.
We rushed to the hospital — unprepared, half-aware, carrying the wrong papers and the wrong confidence.

I was only 33 weeks along.

Steroids to rush my baby's lungs into growing faster than nature planned.
A belt tight around my waist, to monitor baby heartrate.

Two days on a bed with my legs raised, staring at the ceiling, my mind strangely blank.
Fear does that.
It makes you numb.

I was still working. Still taking calls. Still pretending nothing had slipped out of control.

After 48 hours, they took me to the OT.
It was raining heavily outside.

My baby was born through a C-section.
I saw her for a second.
Then she was gone.

She went to the NICU.
I went to a ward.

One floor apart — and worlds away.

My body had delivered, but my heart hadn't caught up.

Three hours after surgery, I coordinated my last office interview — stitches burning, everyone including me acting like this was just another day.

But at midnight, when the lights dimmed and everyone slept, it hit me.

I could barely walk, but I climbed the stairs anyway.
I stood beside her incubator and cried — quietly, fully, finally.

She weighed 1.4 kilos.
For ten days, my world shrank to machines, prayers, and whispered lullabies.

I pumped milk.
I held her skin-to-skin.
I sang "Chanda hai tu… mera taara hai tu" while watching wires breathe for her.

Pain from my stitches didn't matter.
Nothing mattered except her.

When she came home, her clothes hung off her tiny body, like they belonged to another child.

At home, my elder daughter watched me.
She didn't say much at first.

Then, one day, she spoke.

She said she wanted to send her baby sister back to the hospital.
Or back inside my tummy — so she could have her mother again.

When we gently told her that if her sister went back, she might never get to see her again, she fell silent.
Then she walked up, wrapped her tiny arms around her baby sister, and held her tight — rejecting her own wish in an instant.

But that…
That is a story for another time.

I stayed strong until my baby was stable.

And then my body collapsed.

Weight dropped. Sleep disappeared. Food lost meaning.
Panic arrived without warning.

And the hardest truth of all —
I felt distant from the baby I had begged God to save.

It was the paediatricians who said it first.
You need to see your doctor.

Postpartum.
This time, I didn't argue with it.

I called my village — my mother, my mother-in-law, my help, my husband, my elder child who had already grown older than her years.

It took four months to come back to myself.

Postpartum doesn't repeat the same way.
But if you've had it once, your body remembers.

What changed this time wasn't my strength.

It was my awareness.
I wasn't weak.
I wasn't failing.

My body was speaking — asking for love, care, and support.

And this time,
I listened.

MOTHER'S WALL

Dr. Arti

Dr. Sakshi

Mrs. Divya

Mrs. Aradhana

Dr. Pragya

Mrs.Aniie

Mrs. Jiggyassa

Mrs. Shreya

Mrs.Neha

Mrs. Shreya K

Mrs. Anupama

Anonymous

1. Nothing Prepared Me for What Came After

I still remember the moment my daughter was born. Holding her for the first time was the most beautiful feeling I have ever known. Nothing prepares you for that love. But slowly, reality settled in. I was a working professional, used to long days at the office, and suddenly my world revolved around a tiny human who needed me all the time.

What no one prepared me for was postpartum. No one explained how heavy it could feel, or how easily tears would come without reason. My daughter barely slept during her early years, and neither did I. Asking for help didn't feel like an option—I had to manage on my own.

That first year, my career quietly stepped aside. Every bit of strength I had went into caring for my child and learning how to become a mother, one exhausted day at a time.

Those days were challenging, marked by overwhelming moments amid sleepless nights and quiet tears. Yet in that space, I discovered myself—stronger, gentler, deeply devoted. Today, holding my daughter close and watching her grow, I know every sacrifice and career pause led me to becoming a MOTHER—the greatest gift of my life.

- *Aradhana Syal, New Delhi*

@syalaradhana

2. When Feeding Felt Like Failure

In the first six months, I had somehow equated breastfeeding with motherhood itself. So, when my supply was insufficient, and my own paediatrician told me to "sit like the Buddha for eight hours and feed," even comparing me to another new mother, I felt exposed and humiliated.

I was unprepared for how hard breastfeeding would be — or for the stigma wrapped around it. I tried everything: direct feeds, breast pumps (they do help), and eventually formula. Giving formula felt like failure, almost like an insult.

That phase was deeply traumatic, until I slowly understood something simple and freeing: *fed is best.* With time and space, a mother and her little one find their own rhythm — precious and uniquely theirs.

Motherhood cannot be boxed into rules or expectations. A mother doesn't arrive fully formed; she grows, alongside her child.

- *Anupama Narayanan, Chennai*

3. I Needed You There

Six days and nights without sleep broke my body before I even realised it. My partner was caring, trying to make everything right after the pregnancy. Yet his demanding job left little space for what I needed most — emotional presence.

I could see him doing everything to make me comfortable, but my heart was aching for love, for affection, for a shoulder to lean on. That absence hurt more than the exhaustion.

Postpartum emotions are overwhelming. They don't just need help — they need quiet time with your partner, moments where your thoughts can settle and your connection feels whole again.

Our parents' generation lived differently. Their ways, their advice, their expectations came from another time. Even friends couldn't give me the peace I was searching for.

What I needed wasn't solutions or strength. I needed to feel held — mentally, emotionally, gently — while I was falling apart and learning to become a mother.

- *Shreya Rani, Noida*

@ ek_biharibahuria

4. Natural, But Not Easy

Postpartum is one of the most overlooked phases of motherhood. We often assume that once the delivery is over, the hardest part is done, but for many women, that is when the real struggle truly begins.

As both a mother and an obstetrician, I have always strongly advocated for exclusive breastfeeding, and I followed that path with both of my daughters. However, the first time was far from easy. I faced significant physical recovery challenges and a level of exhaustion that was beyond words. Breastfeeding did not come naturally; it was a journey marked by pain, tears, and quiet self-doubt.

With time and perseverance, it did get easier for both my baby and me. But that experience made me realize how unprepared and unsupported most mothers are during this transition. Breastfeeding may be natural, but it is also a learned skill. Learning requires patience, reassurance, and compassion—not the judgment or lack of empathy so many women face.

Mothers need more structured support, not pressure. They need understanding, not guilt. It is time we normalize seeking help and treat the postpartum phase with the clinical and emotional importance it truly deserves.

- ***Dr. Arti Sharma, Bengaluru***

@ dr.arti.s

5. I Could Be Both

I am a dentist.

Before I became a mother,
I was a woman waiting—
seven long years, PCOD,
endless appointments,
prayers whispered into silence,
heartbreaks carried quietly.

And then—Myrah.
A daughter.
A sunrise I had almost stopped
expecting.

Motherhood was beautiful, yes, but it also made me feel smaller than I ever imagined. Dependent. Left behind.
Watching the world rush forward while I stood still,
holding a miracle in my arms
and losing pieces of myself along the way.

The day I chose to step out again, guilt sat heavy on my chest.
How could I leave her, even for a moment?

Then love stepped in.
My husband stepped back so I could step forward—
carrying school runs, routines, and the weight of everyday life,
so I could carry my dreams again.

I walked into my MDS , not as the woman motherhood had shaken, but as someone rising— steadier, stronger, remembering who she was before and becoming someone new.

Motherhood didn't bind me.
It taught me - I could be both.

- ***Dr. Pragya, Patna***
  @Rai ji ki ladki

6. The Day I Chose Presence

When my daughter was born, the early months felt manageable.

Everything changed when I returned to work after eight months—no nanny, no help, just my husband and me.

We split the day.
I started my day at 4 a.m., and returned home by noon.

Then, my husband used to leave for the office.
We only exchanged the baby—no conversations which got limited to chats and calls

Most mornings, she woke without me.
When I came home, she crawled toward me at full speed, eyes sparkling—like she'd found something she'd lost.
I cried every day, questioning myself.

After months, I chose to step away.
Two full years with her—every moment.
I saw the difference in her eyes, her laughter, her calm.

I never regretted it.
When remote work arrived, I returned.

Today, I'm a mother of two—

carrying both choices with quiet certainty.

- *Divya Dubey, Bengaluru*

7. Travel Came with Terms and Conditions

We got married in college, so only recently did we get the chance to travel abroad, see the world, and experience a little luxury. By then, we had a daughter. My first international trip was alone with my 7-month-old on a 13-hour flight to Spain; my husband had flown earlier for a conference. That day I cried, laughed, questioned my existence, and thought of giving up, all within hours. I held her for almost the entire flight, couldn't eat or use the loo, and missed my connecting flight in Germany by six minutes while running with her tied to my chest. I cried alone at the airport, exhausted and overwhelmed.

Spain was special; I'm an architect, and it felt surreal to finally see buildings I had studied for years. But motherhood changed the terms and conditions of my dreams. Even as I stood there, I felt a strange FOMO—I was finally at these iconic landmarks, but I was moving slowly, dropping plans, and breastfeeding instead of exploring. I was there, yet I felt like I was missing out on the "real" experience.

And now, when I travel without her for work, I miss her so much it hurts. The guilt of leaving her behind to follow my own heart feels just as heavy as the exhaustion of carrying her with me. It's a constant tug-of-war: when she's with me, I crave my freedom, and the moment I'm free to chase my dreams, I just want to be back with her. Motherhood changed the map of my heart forever; no matter where I am, a part of me is always somewhere else

- *Shreya K Takkalki, Bengaluru*

	@the_muscle_momma

8. I Thought He Didn't Need Me

My son was born underweight and given this was my first experience holding a child so small, it was overwhelming to have someone depend completely on you for his survival. Since he couldn't latch properly, he was on top feed and it would kill me inside with this pressure of not being able to feed my child with my milk and what if the bond between us did not grow.

Also, because of the postpartum I used to be generally irritated and even the smallest negative comment from anyone would make me cry... one night, my son who was barely a month old, started crying at night, I fed him his bottle, but it didn't help, my Japa got up and came and as soon as she held him, he stopped crying...

While I should have been happy seeing him stop crying, I burst out crying feeling that my son is comfortable is someone else's arms and not mine, that he does not feel connected to me... I sobbed all night but now when I look back, I feel proud of having developed a great bond with my son.

Motherhood is beyond just giving birth or feeding your child... it is about spending both quality and quantity time with your child to develop a strong bond.

- *Anonymous, Kolkata*

9. Twice Chosen, Never Ready

I never believed I was made for marriage or motherhood. I didn't feel maternal, didn't feel ready, didn't even feel curious. But society has a way of deciding for you. So, I became a wife. And then a mother. Twice.

Motherhood, for me, began with fear — fear of responsibility, fear of not knowing how to care for someone so completely. It changed me, whether I wanted it to or not. I became more responsible. More aware. My patience grew.

And yet, I still wouldn't call myself patient.

I love my children, but I won't romanticise the journey. Motherhood didn't transform me into someone soft and instinctive. It taught me to show up even when I doubted myself — and to live inside contradictions without needing to resolve them.

- *G. Annie Sujitha, Mexico*

@ 1814_annie

10. THE STRUGGLE

The hardest part of my first year of motherhood wasn't sleepless nights. It was doing everything alone — without permission to fall apart. We were a nuclear family. Every morning my husband left for work and the house went silent. No extra hands. No one to hold the baby for a minute while I breathed.

My son came early — eight months, just 1.6 kgs. Tiny, fragile, always on the edge of worry. Vaccinations were delayed, immunity was weak, and doctors warned that even a small infection could set him back. So no maids, no cooks, no outside help. Anyone could carry germs. Anyone could be a risk.

So I became everything — mother, nurse, cleaner, cook, guard, and sometimes even a scientist trying to calculate how to keep him safe. For six months, I didn't step out. I cooked during naps, cleaned while watching his chest rise and fall, and ate whenever I remembered. Some days were sunset meals. Some days were no meals. I washed my hands until they cracked. I was scared to cough. Scared to get tired. Tired mothers don't get days off.

People say, "You should rest after delivery." But rest felt like a luxury meant for women with support. My world reduced to four walls and fear that never slept. When I finally came out of that year alive, one thing became clear: the hardest part wasn't the work or the fear — it was motherhood without a support system.

- *Jiggyassa Soni, Mumbai*

  @sweetjiggi

11. When the Fog Lifted

In those early days after my delivery, it was just my husband and

me—a quiet, nuclear household that suddenly felt very loud and very lonely with a newborn. When my husband had to return to work, the days and nights stretched endlessly. I was struggling more than I had ever imagined — postpartum depression, mastitis, and constant breastfeeding challenges made me feel fragile and overwhelmed. That's when support arrived from the most unexpected place. My Jhapa - Madhuri didi - the full-time help who came to assist me with the baby, became so much more than help. She became my anchor. She stayed awake with me through long, exhausting nights. When I broke down, she offered her shoulder without judgment. She reassured me when I doubted myself and stood by me when I felt completely alone. In those moments, she felt nothing short of God-sent—a quiet, steady presence who mothered the mother. Seven years later, she is still with us, still a part of our lives, and I remain deeply grateful for the love and care she gave me during my most vulnerable phase. That experience taught me something profound: sometimes, the strongest bonds aren't formed by blood, but by compassion. By people who step in unexpectedly and hold you up when you didn't even know how to ask for help. Those relationships stay with you forever. Emotionally, it softened me. It allowed me to accept help without guilt and to recognise vulnerability not as weakness, but as honesty. I stopped chasing perfection and started valuing presence, healing, and survival.

- ***Dr. Saakshi Gulati, Chennai***

  @seatback_upright

12. A Letter to the Mother in Dark

Dear Me,

It's 3:14 a.m. I'm sitting on the nursery floor because I don't have the energy to climb back into bed. The baby has finally—finally—stopped crying, but the silence feels louder than the noise did.

I thought this year would be about "firsts." First smile. First step. I thought I'd be tired but glowing, like everyone says. Instead, I feel like I'm wearing someone else's life, like a coat that's too big, and I keep tripping over it.

The moment that shook me wasn't a crisis. It wasn't a fever or a fall. It was the moment I looked at the rocking chair and realized I didn't want to get back in it. I felt a flash of resentment so sharp it made me gasp, followed immediately by a wave of guilt so cold it made me shiver.

I cried because I realized that the "me" who existed before—the one who slept until noon, who finished books in one sitting, who knew exactly who she was—wasn't just hiding. She was gone. And you weren't sure if you liked the person who had replaced her.

Here is what I wish I could tell you in that darkness:

The "Motherhood Instinct" isn't a constant hum; it's a radio signal. Sometimes it's clear, and sometimes it's just static. That doesn't mean you're doing it wrong.

Love and Exhaustion can live in the same room. You can adore that tiny human with a ferocity that scares you and still desperately wish for an hour where nobody touches you.

The "Glow" is often just sweat. And that's okay.

That night on the floor changed me quietly. It was the night I stopped trying to be the "perfect" mother I have imagined and started being the real mother my baby actually has. I traded the performance for the presence. When the sun comes up, I will drink lukewarm coffee and find a way to laugh again. The coat will start to fit. Not because it got smaller, but because I grew into it.

Hang in there, fighter. You're doing better than you think.

- ***Neha Sharma, U.A.E.***

  @neha_kumar.sharma2201

ABOUT THE AUTHOR

Hi, I'm Pallavi — a mother, a lawyer by training, a writer by instinct, and a lifelong learner who is still figuring things out one snack box, breakdown, and small breakthrough at a time.

I'm not a "perfect mom."

Just a next-door mother who has lived the real, unfiltered version of postpartum — the exhaustion, the guilt, the tenderness, the quiet victories, and the slow return to herself.

My experience with postpartum depression after my first daughter reshaped how I understood motherhood. It stripped away glossy ideals and replaced them with something far more honest — a deeply human experience that needs compassion, support, and shared language. This book was born from that honesty.

Somewhere along that journey, a deeper question began to form:
How do we create a world that feels gentler — for children growing up in it, and for the mothers raising them?

That question became **Bälamoé.**

The name itself holds what I was searching for.
Bäla, from Sanskrit, means child.
Moé, from Japanese, speaks of affection — a tender, instinctive warmth.

Together, they reflect what I believe childhood — and motherhood — deserve:
care that is playful yet intentional,
love that is soft yet grounding,
and spaces where both children and mothers are held with affection.

Bälamoé began not as a brand, but as a feeling — the desire to design childhood with thoughtfulness, while never forgetting the woman doing the nurturing.

I hope this book feels less like advice and more like company — a friend sitting beside you, quietly reminding you:

You're not alone.
You're not failing.
You're doing better than you think.

Because in the end, I'm just a mother like you —
learning, evolving, creating, and becoming along the way.

Please join our community and make it stronger - **@balamoemoms**

Reach us out at: letsconnect@balamoe.in

A Note Before You Close the Book

If you're looking for a neat ending,
motherhood doesn't offer one.

There is no moment where everything settles for good.
No day where you wake up certain, finished, or complete.

What does change—slowly, quietly—is awareness.

You begin to notice when something isn't right.
You stop brushing exhaustion aside.
You recognise that asking for help is not failure, but wisdom.

This book doesn't give instructions.
It offers recognition.
For days when you feel capable and grounded.
And for days when you don't.

If some pages felt uncomfortably familiar,
that was intentional.
Motherhood is not meant to be carried alone.
And survival should not require silence.

This is not the end of the work.
It's the point where attention begins.

There are more conversations ahead.
They will unfold when they're ready.

For now, let this be enough.

If these pages made you pause, breathe, or feel less alone,
carry that with you.

The rest will meet you in time.

ACKNOWLEDGEMENT

This book was born in the in-between moments — between feeds and fatigue, between love and loss of self, between who I was and who I was becoming.

To my children, who unknowingly became my greatest teachers. You arrived without manuals and rewrote every belief I had about strength, patience, and love. This book exists because of you — not despite you.

To my partner, for standing beside me through the visible and invisible shifts. For the days you held space, and even for the days you didn't know how — both shaped this journey.

To the women who spoke honestly — in whispers, late-night messages, half-finished sentences, and quiet breakdowns — thank you for trusting me with your truth. This book carries pieces of your stories, too.

To mothers everywhere who are doing the work without applause, without clarity, and often without help — this is for you. If these pages make you feel seen, even for a moment, then they have done their job.

And finally, to myself — for staying, for questioning, for writing when it would have been easier to disappear into survival mode. This book is proof that even in the probation year, growth is already happening.

You were never failing.
You were learning.

— Pallavi Raj

FEW TERMS that might have intrigued you!

Godh Bharai (Noun)

Etymology: Hindi; Godh (lap) + Bharai (to fill).

A traditional Indian ceremony, often likened to a baby shower, performed during the third trimester of pregnancy to celebrate the impending arrival of a child and to honor the mother-to-be as a vessel of new life. Unlike its modern Western counterparts which often focus on the infant's needs, Godh Bharai is an ancient rite of passage centered on the spiritual and emotional fortification of the mother. It is a ceremony of symbolic abundance. The mother-to-be is dressed in ceremonial finery—typically a vibrant silk saree and floral or gold jewellery—and seated in a place of honor.

Upma (Noun)

Etymology: Derived from the South Indian words Uppu (salt) and Maavu (flour/meal).

Definition: A traditional savory porridge originating from South India, crafted from dry-roasted semolina (coarse wheat) and tempered with a complex array of spices, lentils, and aromatics. It is celebrated for its duality: simple enough for a quick weekday meal, yet sophisticated enough to be served at South Indian weddings. It is the ultimate comfort food—a warm, savory embrace that marks the beginning of the day for millions.

Sabudana Khichdi (Noun)

Etymology: Hindi; Sabudana (Sago/Tapioca pearls) + Khichdi (a dish of mixed ingredients).

Definition: A gluten-free, carbohydrate-rich pilaf made from soaked tapioca pearls, toasted peanuts, and potatoes. It is the quintessential "fasting food" (Vrat ka Khana) in Hindu culture. It serves as an instant energy booster for those observing a fast, transforming a period of abstinence into a culinary indulgence. It is a staple of street food culture in regions like Maharashtra, where it is served hot in paper bowls to morning commuters.

Jhapa (Noun)

Etymology: Derived from Hindi; refers to the period of postpartum confinement and care. A traditional 40-to-60-day recovery period following childbirth, during which a new mother and her infant remain in seclusion to prioritize healing, bonding, and the establishment of breastfeeding. Jhapa is based on the ancient Ayurvedic belief that a woman is "reborn" after giving birth, leaving her body delicate and "cold." The practice is a holistic support system that shifts all domestic and childcare burdens away from the mother, allowing her to focus entirely on her own restoration. Traditionally managed by the mother's own mother or a Jhapa Maid (a specialized postpartum doula), this period is defined by warmth, nutrition, and touch. In this book, Jhapa Maid has been referred to as Jhapa for simplicity.

Few Other Terms:

- Burper: Author coined term for someone having expertise in giving burp to infants (Burp: A postnatal care technique involving the gentle rhythmic patting or stroking of an infant's back to assist in the expulsion of ingested air from the stomach)
- Aapka Paani Madam : "Here's your glass of water, ma'am"

- Aur aap kahenge, aapne bataya nai: “And, You will say, You didn’t tell me about this!”
- Didi, aap baitho: “Ma’am, you please have a seat”
- Papa, kabhi kitchen mein nai gaye the : “My father had hardly stepped into the kitchen ever”

DISCLAIMER

Nature of the Work: This book, "You're Hired, Mommy! The Probation Year" is a work of creative expression. It's a compilation of personal reflections, fictionalized narratives, and contributed stories regarding the journey of motherhood. The contents of this book are for informational, emotional resonance and storytelling purposes only. It is not a self-help guide, a parenting manual, or a clinical resource.

No Professional Advice (Medical & Legal): The author writes this work solely in a personal and creative capacity as a mother and author. Nothing in this book constitutes legal or medical advice.

- **Medical/Mental Health:** The narratives within—including those touching upon postpartum depression (PPD), physical health, childcare, etc. —reflect personal, circumstantial choices and subjective experiences. They are not a substitute for professional medical diagnosis, advice, or treatment. Always seek the advice of a qualified healthcare provider regarding mental health or medical conditions.
- **Legal:** No attorney-client relationship is formed by the purchase or reading of this book. The views expressed are personal and do not represent legal opinions or interpretations of the law.

Section I: Fictionalized Narratives The characters and the events in the first section are works of fiction. While inspired by the author's real-life experiences and those of other mothers, names, characters, places, and incidents are products of the author's imagination. Any resemblance to actual persons, living or dead, or actual events is purely coincidental.

The video/film/image for @Sneha.Rohan.Diaries contains AI-generated content. All characters, faces, and visuals within this production are artificial and have been generated or significantly altered using artificial intelligence tools. This work is intended for entertainment purposes only and is a demonstration of AI's potential in filmmaking.

All depicted characters, likenesses, performances, and any derivative representations are fictional. Any resemblance to real persons, living or dead, is purely coincidental.

All characters, likenesses, and derivative representations are claimed by Kaushvika Soulcraft Creation Private Limited to the extent permitted under applicable law.

Section II: Contributed Stories & Consent The second section contains real-life accounts submitted by twelve individual contributors and one by the author herself.

- **Consent:** Proper legal consent was obtained from all contributors for the publication of their stories. Formal records of this consent, including the approval of final edited versions, are maintained by the publisher.
- **Anonymity:** To respect the privacy of the individuals involved, one contributor has chosen to share their story under the condition of anonymity. All other stories are attributed as per the contributors' express permission.
- **Views Expressed:** The views, thoughts, opinions and experiences shared in these stories are those of the respective contributors and do not necessarily reflect the views of the author or the publisher.

Limitation of Liability: To the extent permissible under applicable laws of India, the author and publisher disclaim any liability for any adverse effects, loss, or damage resulting from the use or application of the information contained in this book. By choosing to read this book, the reader acknowledges that they do so at their own discretion and risk.

Jurisdiction: This disclaimer and all matters relating to this book shall be governed by the laws of India. Any legal proceedings arising out of or in connection with this work shall be subject to the exclusive jurisdiction of the courts in Mumbai, India.

www.ingramcontent.com/pod-product-compliance
Ingram Content Group UK Ltd.
Pitfield, Milton Keynes, MK11 3LW, UK
UKHW041348190726
13845UKWH00026B/499

9 788199 620100